WILDERNESS

WOMEN

Live to tell the Story

Wilderness Women: Live to tell the story

Published by Edmond Emehel Groupe, LLC © 2009

Printed in the United States of America

Unless otherwise indicated, Scripture quotations from *The Holy* Bible, New International Version

© 1973, 1984 by International Bible Society

Also quoted:

New American Standard Bible (NASB)

© 1960, 1977 by the Lockman Foundation

The Amplified Bible

© 1965 by Zondervan Publishing House

WILDERNESS

WOMEN

Live to tell the Story

Printed in the United States of America
ISBN 978-0-578-02433-2

What people are saying about
Wilderness Women: Live to tell the story

"I love this book! The stories are powerful and really prick the emotions. I commend Toni Emehel for the wonderful way she reached out to other women to bring together a collection of powerful tales of everyday life. The possibilities are endless for this nicely done work!"

—Pat Gadsden
Founder/Publisher Women-Connect Magazine
Harrisburg, Pennsylvania

"Congratulations to the authors of "Wilderness Women." If there's ever been a time to encourage the soul and spirit now is the time. *Wilderness Women* intricately weaves the real life stories of uncertain and life altering circumstances of women and their testimonies of victory and triumph through faith in God. My wife and I are certain that lives will be encouraged and transformed through the transparent stories of the "Wilderness Women."

—Pastor Michael and Lady Sharon Stevens
University City COGIC
Charlotte, North Carolina

"Wilderness Women: Live to tell the story," book and symposium were both an educational and enlightening experience for me. The symposium caused me to do much self-reflection and encouraged me to have fun as I claim the power that lies within me. Thank you, "Wilderness Women" for sharing your stories of love, endurance and self-empowerment!"

— Geraldine Walker
Harrisburg, Pennsylvania

"Excellent job ladies! I had an opportunity to experience your spellbinding workshop and oral presentation of the book during the women's history celebration at the State Museum of Pennsylvania. The thought provoking tribute to "every woman" that was performed by co-author Jacqueline Guess was very touching and delved deep down in the issues that we as women share. This is the type of book and workshop that should be ministered to women and young adolescent girls all over the country. Again, job well done ladies!"

—Willie Campbell,
CEO, P&W Associates
Germantown, Maryland

"I would like to say thank you to the "Wilderness Women" for writing and sharing their heartfelt stories. There were many healing words for the soul, and I am sure every woman can relate to at least a couple of the wilderness experiences that these sisters had to endure through their wilderness journey. As a woman, I have found that when difficult times become too hard for me to handle alone, I tend to vibrate towards love, because I know my strength and power lies in being centered with God, who gives me peace of mind."

—Mary Swanson
Harrisburg, Pennsylvania

Dedication

To my daughters, Jessica Laneé, Tressica Denise and Madison Oluchi: each of you are marked for greatness and destined to accomplish great works in this world. Be steadfast and knowledgeable of your original design, which will ultimately lead you to an empowered life; lived in purpose and in alignment with the *Word* of God.

Hugs and kisses,

Mom

Welcome to *Wilderness Women: Live to tell the story.*

This life transforming anthology brings together essential rudiments of life, including the infallible *Word* of God and the powerful message of *His* wholeness through healing. It is essential that you know how to use this book in order for you to receive its full benefit. There are three important areas of this book that I would like to acquaint you with. The first area is the *"Contributing Authors"* section. This is the section which lists all of the authors who contributed personal testaments of wilderness situations experienced in their private lives. I encourage you to get to know these courageous women as they have been appointed to guide you through the wilderness process for the purpose of revealing all that God has in store for you from the reading of this book. You will note that each contributing author has availed herself of any title, professional acumen, education and/or social status; for these things do not bear witness to whom she is in Christ Jesus.

There is an area in the book that I would truly hate for you to miss entitled, *"The Wilderness Woman Experience."* This section is situated immediately before you get to the written testaments. This segment of the book will give a better understanding of the unmasking each of the "Wilderness Women" had to undergo in order to be a part of the "Wilderness Woman Project." This was not my requirement, rather God's requirement so that each woman would be rightly positioned for an outpouring of *His Spirit.*

Finally, you will encounter manna from heaven embodied in the compilation of *"Testaments"* written by the "Wilderness Women." Each testament ends with a brief annotation entitled, *"Pressing the Mark."* These annotations are written by me and have been drawn through prayer and personal Bible study. They are intended to speak to your spirit and enhance the success of your escape from wilderness situations affecting your life.

It is an exhilarating experience to see men and women healed and set free through the power of testimony. It is my earnest prayer that your wholeness will increase as a result of coming in contact with, *Wilderness Women: Live to tell the story.*

With *His* love,

Toni Emehel

Contents

I solemnly pray that this life transforming anthology will bless you immensely.

—Toni Emehel

Author's Note

The challenge of casting contributing authors for *Wilderness Women: Live tell the story* was tremendous. It was a process weighted by an undeniable burden to craft a life to literature anthology that extends far beyond the natural. More than 125 women were invited to take part in this inverted process by which each woman's life experiences deemed her suitability to journey with the project. The rest is, as they say, "herstory" intimately expressed by the unique moments captured from each woman's life.

As you enter into the private lives of these nine courageous women, who through soul searching and pain have managed to capture life on a few pages of words, realize that each woman's narrative is an individual expression of her love for God. Each author has her own vernacular expressed through her own vigor of words, intonation and manner.

May this book be a time-honored mark in history that affirms our love for God, our love for *His* people and our love for the Body of Christ.

—Toni E. Emehel

I encourage you to get to know these courageous women as they have been appointed to guide you through the wilderness process for the purpose of revealing all that God has in store for you from the reading of this book.

—Toni Emehel

Contributing Authors

Sadie E. Anderson
V. Arleen
Lydia Hilt Clay
Janie F. Edmond-Reid
Jacqueline Little-Guess
Sheria Lofton
Tina L. Massey
Rosa L. Watson

Sadie E. Anderson, author of *Highway through the Wilderness,* has ministered to the lives of men and women for more than forty years. As a mother of 10 children, Sadie lives a life evident of the Holy Spirit working through her. She is a woman dedicated to touching the hearts of others through ministry. Sadie has a unique ability to minister hope and encouragement no matter the age or stage of life one might be in. Sadie is a sage vessel consecrated for God's use. She lives in the suburbs of Charlotte, North Carolina where Sadie is surrounded by the tender love and care of children who proudly call her blessed. In perilous times, such as these, there is a thirst and hunger for human connection and spiritual direction from model women who exude trust and respect. Sadie is such a woman. Through grace and genuine admonition of the Lord, Sadie delivers insightful biblical perspectives on real issues that impact lives every day.

V. Arleen, author of *Circling the Mountain,* is the youngest of seven children. Born in New Jersey, she currently makes her home in Charlotte, North Carolina. V. has a history of more than 23 years of working with children and families, both secularly and in the body of Christ. A divorcee with no children of her own, she has had the privilege of being a surrogate mother to many. She is an active member of her church's Single Women's Small Group Ministry. V. has a passion for restoring healthy relationships in our communities, as she is both an active intercessor and advocate for this ministry. She has received personal training from God in becoming a woman of prayer, purpose and power. Look for future books and works by V., as she continues her assignment of exposing the lies of the enemy and revealing the truth of God's unfailing love for His own.

Lydia Hill Clay, author of *Letters from the Sands,* is a devoted and loving wife of 19 years, who resides in south Charlotte, North Carolina with her husband, Val Clay, Jr. Lydia compassionately speaks to the hearts of women as she shares the enduring challenges of a long distance relationship. As a role model, she has allowed God to shape the imperfections of her marriage into an enduring relationship without an exit clause. Through her story, Lydia inspires others to love and persevere through distractions and challenges that sometimes take root in long distance relationships. As a product of a close family unit, Lydia passionately encourages others to diligently pursue an intimate relationship with God, invest in the institution of marriage, and find value in the importance of maintaining the family unit.

Janie F. Edmond Reid, author of *Youch! I'm Stuck in a Briar Patch,* is married to her best friend, Kenneth B. Reid. They live just outside of Charlotte, North Carolina in the town of Indian Trail with three of God's highest blessings, Felita (15), Kenneth Jr. (8), and Darryl (6). Janie's comedic approach to addressing some of the toughest marital issues facing families today leaves readers optimistic, challenged and provoked to change. Janie is a real woman whose conversational writing style openly shares real issues in her own marriage, to quickly build an authentic setting that readers can relate to. Through compassion and candor, Janie weaves scriptural truths with personal triumphs and tragedies to deliver a message of hope. Janie is a breath of fresh air sent to help husbands and wives realize that God's divine plan for marriage is within their reach.

Jacqueline Little Guess, author of *To the One I Love(d),* resides in Matthews, North Carolina with her husband and children. She is an invigorating storyteller whose parable writing style creates compelling illustrations that help others relate the word of God to everyday life situations. Jacqueline is an excellent communicator who radiates the joy of Christ in her life. She is a woman inspired by the insightful wisdom of her late mother, Ethel Little, whom Jacqueline dedicates this writing saying, *"Mom, I now understand what you were silently saying."*

Sheria Lofton, author of *Guilt and Shame,* lives in Matthews, North Carolina with the husband of her youth. She is a caring woman of God who possesses great strength and courage. The depth of Sheria's writings connects with the hearts of young and adolescent women and inspires them to wash away the stained tragedies of the past to discover the brilliant glow of God's grace.

Tina L. Massey, author of *The Pain behind the Mask,* is an educator, musician and mother of three; Devona, Tyler and Tristan. She resides in Charlotte, North Carolina. Tina enjoys working behind the scenes to accomplish the work of God. Her passion is working in the ministry of "encouragement and exhortation" to help women in distress by assisting them with picking up the broken pieces of their fractured lives and move ahead for the glory of God. Tina's favorite scripture is Psalms 27, which has been the foundation which has kept her through trial moments.

Rosa L. Watson, author of *Riding the Whirlwind in the Wilderness,* is happily married to Eric G. Watson and proud mother of Antron D. Watson. She resides in Harrisburg, Pennsylvania where she challenges others to look within to discover the glory and power of God. With her gift of encouragement, God uses Rosa as a spiritual guide to support others in their journey to discover their divine purpose. Rosa is a woman who is committed to uplifting others and making positive change within the world as she is guided by God. She dares to believe that God changes lives once we have an authentic encounter with *Him*. Rosa has been described as an angelic presence sent to inspire and enrich lives for the greater good of God. Her words paint vivid pictures to provoke readers to action and empower them with the tools necessary to follow their spiritual calling in life.

The act of rectifying my past wrong seemed honorable, but sadly, it was not biblical.
—*Toni Emehel*

The Wilderness Woman Experience

This project has surely been a *"labor of love"* for the Wilderness Women. I had always heard this phrase in the Christian community and never understood what it really meant, until now. God has a unique way of giving a deeper revelation of this His word through life's experiences and makes clearer those things we heard so often while growing up.

This book has led us on a journey of healing, deliverance and breakthrough that we could not have imagined when we started. God has revealed to some of us our purpose and calling in life, to others He has provoked the books that have been lying dormant in our very spirits; yet to others, He has uncovered areas that were in need of adjustment to come in line with His will. I believe that all of us have developed a new boldness and tenacity, along with the lightness that comes from being released from bondage.

It amazes me how God takes you through the very process that you are called to minister to. He shapes your testimony so you can have first-hand knowledge when He releases you to those to whom you have been called. As the Wilderness Women came together we learned from each other things that were phenomenal, mind transforming and life changing. We realized that learning and revelation never ends, regardless of your age. We know what God has done "first" in us and we rejoice!

Now, we want to see what He will do through us. As you read the pages of this book, it is our prayer that you will find an experience to which you can relate, that will bring about healing, deliverance and breakthrough in your life. We pray that you will be set free from *fear, guilt, doubt, unbelief, pain* and *emotional distress*. It was never God's intent for you to remain in a wilderness state of life. Now is your time to discover the way out! Come on the journey from the wilderness to the *"Promised Land"* with us. Will you journey with us to receive deliverance from the wilderness situations affecting your life today?

We realize that there may be obstacles that you need to overcome in order to join us on this journey. We are sensitive to that, because we too were faced with many obstructions that threatened to barricade our path toward finishing this great work. There were times when some of us thought that we would not make it to the end, while consoling others who were about to buckle in defeat. No doubt about it, we all had to face some giants in completing this project. Yet, we knew and believed within our hearts that God was able to see us through. Just as He always has, God has brought us through the writing of this book with great success! To God be the glory!

It is important to us that we hear how *Wilderness Women: Live to tell the story* has encouraged you. Visit our blog site at www.WildernessWomenSpeak.blogspot.com to share an account of your experience. I personally would love to hear from you!

— V. Arleen

Testaments

As you enter into the private lives of these nine courageous women, who through soul searching and pain have managed to capture life on a few pages of words, realize that each woman's narrative is an individual expression of her love for God. Each author has her own vernacular expressed through her own vigor of words, intonation and manner.

—*Toni Emehel*

To the One I Love(d)

by
Jacqueline Little-Guess

TO THE ONE I LOVE(D)

"And now we have these three things: faith, hope, and love, but love is the greatest of them all."

—1 Corinthians 13:13

August 20, 2008

To: The One I Love(d)

Dear Beloved,

 I hope this letter finds you in the best of physical, emotional and most of all, spiritual health. I know you are surprised to receive this letter from me. You are probably wondering where I have been for so long. How long has it been? Oh yes, 10 ½ years. That is a long time, isn't it? Yes, my body has been here with you, but my spirit has been long gone. You see, I have been on an unchartered and uncivilized trip through the wilderness. Oh, but you should know that already because you are the one that drove and left me here. You left me here to fend for myself. So, I thought you would want to know all about my experience. Sit down, turn the television off and read all about it.

 Before I tell you about my experience, I want to take this opportunity to talk about the vehicle you used to drive me here. Shall we start at the beginning? Yes, I think we should. Remember how you ripped my heart out 10 ½ years ago, leaving me on my own to repair it? You devastated me and took advantage of my trust, which you claim was only because of your curiosity. You really insulted my intelligence with that one! They say, "Curiosity killed the cat." Well, your curiosity not only killed the cat; it killed trust, respect and a great amount of love that was once shared between us. Yes, I know you said you were sorry. But, remember how you so quickly padded your apology by quoting me the scripture on forgiveness? You played with my spiritual emotions like an NFL player on a football field. I call that spiritual manipulation. Doesn't that same bible you like to quote speak about what you did? Why didn't you quote that verse? Remember I was the one that had to try and repair ALL the broken pieces? I had to somehow clean up your mess; to teach forgiveness while trying to learn it myself. Remember how I had to be strong, keep you happy, act as if everything was fine, and most of all keep silent? Remember how you told me not to hold it over your head for the rest of your life? What about my life? Boy, when they say love hurts, they weren't kidding!! Or, was that truly love? And to top it all off, you told me you loved me in the same breath you used to demand your respect as the "man of the house."

Remember how you told me you knew I was hurting? Well if you knew, why didn't you do something about it? The best way for me to describe the magnitude of the wilderness you released me in some years ago, is to create a similar scenario where you are able to walk in my shoes:

****

Imagine I come up to you, smiling and seemingly loving on you as your faithful companion. After I have your complete trust, I pull out a 9mm Luger and shoot you in the middle of your heart. I tell you I am sorry, but I just stand there, smiling, while watching you bleed. I have every expectation for you to clean up your own blood and cover up the wound, once you get over the initial shock, so no one will ever see it. And don't take too long, because we must move on with our lives. There ain't no need to worry about going to the hospital, because God is a healer and in time He will heal you. But, in the meanwhile you need to figure out how to stop the blood that you are still losing. The more blood you lose, the colder you become. Not only are you losing blood, but you are in tremendous pain. I know you are hurting, I can see it all over your face. But, I still don't want to get you the help you need because it might expose me.

I, being annoyed ask you, "What is wrong with you and why have you grown so distant from me?" I know the answer, but refuse to address the issue. So, then I ask you, "When will YOU forgive and forget? Was not my telling you I'm sorry enough?"

Now, I demand that you act as if that unattended wound is not there. Although the shot did not kill you, you have lost a lot of blood, been in great pain and the wound is now infected. The infection is spreading throughout your body and it is making you sick. Eventually you start to care for that wound yourself, but it leaves an ugly scar. More importantly than that, the bullet is still in your heart. Now, it is no longer the wound that is an issue; it is what's in your heart that will eventually kill you.

****

Does that shed some light on how I have been feeling for the last 10 ½ years? That's a long time. Bleeding internally, hurting and silently screaming on the inside to make sure no one heard me. I have been screaming so long that my silent voice has no voice anymore. But I have to protect your good name, your honor. I have become that woman other women talk about. You know the one; she stays in a painful relationship, albeit emotional or physical, it still hurts.

I have to honor my vow, for better or for worse, until death do us part. That is the "Christian" thing to do. I had no idea that the worse would come so soon and last so long. Did you honor your vow to protect me? I trusted you to protect my heart. Through all my pain, even through muffled screams, I did my part for all those years. I lived as though nothing was wrong. I lived a lie. My body was still with you; dressed well, laughing, having the time of its life while trying to keep cover on my deeply inflicted wound.

There were many times I would run to the bathroom and cry in silence because I was hurting so bad. And those sleepless nights when I cried myself to sleep, as you rolled over and turned your back on me, were the most painful. You knew I was hurting, showed no compassion and refused to reach out and help me. The hurt was too much to bear sometimes. The emotional rollercoaster YOU took me on was making me sick, physically. All I asked was that you help me. Help me to understand. I wanted you to talk to me. Just talk to me. You owed me that much.

I can see you frowning up your face as you are reading this, wondering why am I revisiting this issue again? I'm sure you are also wondering why I could not tell you what I have to say face to face. First, a person can't revisit a place where they have never left. And to be honest with you, I have tried to talk to you face to face all to no avail. I have called out to you on so many occasions, but you only heard sounds echoing in the wilderness and never my words. I thought it best this way because now I can express myself without your interruptions trying to explain how you feel. For 10 ½ years it has been about you and your feelings. Remember, I protected your name and honor. Well, who was protecting me? Me?

Finally, it's about me. Since I can't trust you to do it, I am finally thinking of myself. You do remember me don't you? I'm the one you left wandering in the wilderness. Do you know what I look like anymore? Hey, I don't even know what I look like anymore. Is that why you didn't come to rescue me? Because you can't remember what the real me looks like? What happened to my rescue mission? Where were my tracking hounds? Wasn't I worth that much? It's not like you don't know where you left me. Although, I went deep into the wilderness, from time to time I would always come back to the same spot you left me just in case you were there waiting for me. But you never came. You always avoided discussing the issue. Were you too afraid or proud; or maybe you just wanted to leave me here?

Whatever the case, I'm quite sure you are eager to hear about my wilderness experience. After all, you are the one who created this wilderness environment for me. Believe me, it was an experience not an adventure. Do you have any idea what it is like in the wilderness? Contrary to what you might believe, it is not lonely there. When I had emotional parties, distrust came and partied with me. When the nights were cold, shame blanketed me, while pain fanned me when the days were hot. My tears would wash me as rage would dry me off. Depression would massage my temples when I had a headache as resentment massaged my feet. When I was thirsty, hatred would soothe my parched tongue as hurt would comb my hair with the thorns of deception. For 10 1/2 years I nibbled on the seed of bitterness, watered by the wine of anger, which has taken root and has now become a full grown tree. Have you ever tried to pull a tree root up with your bare hands? Look at my hands and see the results. Do you know what it is like to have roots choking the life out of you; or better yet, can you imagine someone or something choking off the fruit your tree was destined to bear? I don't think you can.

I do have a confession to make. While in the wilderness, I had a love affair. He, unlike you, was so easy to talk to. He took one look at me and saw my pain. He knew about my silent screaming. My lover showed me things about myself that I didn't even know. He hung on my every word, never interrupting me when I told him how I was feeling. He never frowned when I talked to him; he just smiled and told me he understood. He knew how to whisper in my ear and tell me everything I wanted to hear. He had gotten into my head.

We became a part of each other. He convinced me you were never coming to rescue me and that he was the only one that really loved me. I believed him. He promised he would always be by my side and he kept his word. Every time heartache would come, he would rush to my side and soothe me. To keep me alive, he was the one that fed me the seeds of bitterness. My lover allowed me to lay my head on his big broad shoulders and when I was too weak, he would cradle me in his big strong arms and carry me deeper into the wilderness. Then he would tell me that as long as I stayed with him, I would feel less pain. I clung to him so tight because I felt he was all I had. He had captured my heart. When he had my complete trust, (just as you once did) we began to drink the wine of anger. I became so intoxicated that I allowed him to impregnate me. I knew then I had gone too far. I knew I could not bear his offspring and I could not let anyone see the fruit of my affair. This seed had to be aborted. I tried to break free but his captivating aroma paralyzed me. My lover, whose name is Unforgiveness, vowed never to let me go.

As I struggled to end the love affair, I had a dream that I was soaring through the air towards Heaven. As I was approaching Heaven, there was one specific cloud that I kept my eye on. It grabbed my attention because it looked like a big soft smiley face. The closer I got to the cloud, the more I could see it was taking on the form of a man. By the time I was almost to the point of touching this cloud, everything but the face had completely formed. While smiling, the cloud reached out his hand to me and the feeling of peace I had, could never in this lifetime be explained. As I reached my hand out to grab his, I noticed his face was beginning to form more and my peaceful feeling went to another level. But, before I could grab his hand and before his face was completely formed, he quickly faded away and I was left suspended in air.

That dream left questions running though my mind. Did I really die that night? Did the cloud fade away because it was not my time yet? Or did it fade because God, being merciful, was allowing me to give thought to the questions; What if I go to sleep and my physical body never wakes up, where would my soul wake up? Are there unresolved issues in my heart I need to take care of before I can grab that cloud's hand? My answer: I had to somehow let my lover go.

As time went on, Unforgiveness carried me out of the wilderness into the next level, a very cold place. He was right when he told me I would feel less pain. As soon as we got to the edge of this place, my body started to go numb because it was so cold. The further we got into this dark, cold and dismal place, the more feeling I lost in my body. This was a place that everything appeared normal but was hard and cold to the touch. Although it was so cold, the stench of death was so strong. My heart was getting colder and colder, which I knew would eventually lead to death. I had enough feeling left to know this was not a place I wanted to be in, nor was I ready to die. The wilderness was nothing compared to this place, which I eventually found out was The Petrified Forest. My dream started to become more real to me. Even though I had lost my silent voice, I still had just enough of a whimper to ask God to help me. I had had enough. It was time to come home. I needed God's help more than ever before.

So you see I had to write you this letter to let you know although I am a little dusty, bruised and battered, I am on my way back home where I belong. I miss my family and the 10 ½ years of my life that I have spent wandering in the wilderness and I am tired. Oh, don't worry I'm no longer waiting for you to come. I understand now I have to do this without you.

I still have some miles to go until I get home. I am at the edge of the wilderness and I can see civilization now. I can hear the cars go by and smell the fresh air again. You know what's funny? Civilization was right there all the time but I could not hear the cars because Unforgiveness was whispering in my ear. Nor could I smell the fresh air because of his captivating aroma.

I cannot tell you that everything is perfect because it's not. It has been a constant battle with my ex-lover. Every now and then I can still smell a hint of his aroma blowing in the wind. I know the only way to rid myself of him is to kill him. Once I began to write this letter I could see him weakening. He no longer looks as handsome to me as he did before and he no longer has those strong arms and broad shoulders to cradle me when I'm feeling weak.

Imagine the heartache I could have saved myself if I had only done this 10 ½ years ago. But that is in the past. I also must detoxify my body of the wine of anger and also kill the root that the seed of bitterness has produced. Writing you this letter is one of many steps I am taking to accomplish this. I had to let you know how I have been feeling for so many years. I had to let you know about the silent screaming, the lover, the hurt and everything else that went with it. I am coming home. So don't be surprised if real soon you look and see ME standing there.

See ya soon,

The one that love (d) you

(PS: I was thinking, perhaps you did not come back to the wilderness to get me because you are lost in a wilderness of your own. When I get home will YOU be there?)

PRESSING THE MARK

by Toni Emehel

It is very easy to stumble upon the spiritual poison of unforgiveness while wandering in the wilderness of a broken heart. The aroma of bitterness and betrayal permeates the air and comforts the body like a warm gentle breeze. When left unattended an encounter with spiritual poison can spread throughout the body as illustrated by the foregoing narrative. Even after 10 ½ years, it is never too late to heal the wounds, cure the scars and repair the damage of a broken heart that has been drained empty.

God provided the world with the perfect example of how natural it should be to forgive when *HE* sent *HIS* word, Jesus Christ to dwell among us. Jesus experienced the pain of betrayal, slander, malice and broken relationships that could have easily resulted in a hell-bound condition of unforgiveness. In the end, Jesus died of a broken heart, crying out to God to forgive those who had sinned against *HIM*. While forgiveness can not erase history, it will dictate your future. Once we learn how to cleanse our spiritual cavities of the poison stemming from unforgiveness, we can refocus our attention on the redemptive power of God and allow it to heal our hearts and minds. It is then, and only then that we can receive *HIS* comfort to fill the emptiness within us that was once filled with the infection of unforgiveness. At that point, we can freely love *HIM*.

PONDERING THOUGHTS

Unforgiveness is a sin that inhibits you from fulfilling God's commandment of loving one another, for it is impossible to love one whom you are unable to forgive. The Lords Prayer (Matthew 6:9-13) admonishes God to forgive us as we have forgiven those who trespass against us. How comfortable are you with this?

I began to see with "new eyes" and hear with "new ears"

—*Rosa L. Watson*

Riding the Whirlwind in the Wilderness

by
Rosa L. Watson

RIDING THE WHIRLWIND
IN THE WILDERNESS

"For many are called, but few are chosen."

—*Matthew 24:14*

I believe that prior to birth each of us has been given a mission to accomplish while we are on this earth. I believe that the people who are apart of our lives have been placed there by God for the specific purpose to help us on our journey through life to accomplish our mission. Strategically placed along the road, they remind us *"where we came from"*, *"where we are headed"*, and *"what we are supposed to do when we get there"*. There are also times, while traveling on the road, that we feel that we are all alone. Especially when it is cold and dark and the winds of life begin to stir up all kinds of debris, whipping around us, making it hard to see our way and sometimes inflicting blows that can be staggering as we walk against the wind. I call those times, the *"whirlwinds of the wilderness"*. Some of us have been casualties of the whirlwinds - either severely injured rendered unable to travel any further, in dire need of aid or lost and disoriented, not knowing which way to go. Then, there are those who have suffered a fatal blow from the debris of the storm, never to reach their destination. I will share with you my story of how I learned to *"ride the whirlwind"* and use the force of the wind to propel me further on my journey to accomplish my mission.

I was born the seventh child to my parents, Willie and Sadie. Unlike my six siblings before me and the five after me, my mother gave birth to me at home with the help of a midwife. There I was, already doing things differently by not being born in a hospital. But, being born the seventh child on the seventh day of the week (Saturday), automatically meant that there was something divine about my being here.

My parents were professed Christians: saved, sanctified, baptized and filled with the Holy Ghost. My father, whom I affectionately call "Daddy", is now deceased. He was a devoted Deacon whose name is engraved in the cornerstone of Mount Livingstone United Holy Church in Selma, North Carolina, a church he helped to build from the ground up. Daddy took pride in all that he did for his family and the church, as it was not uncommon for him to prepare a meal for the family or pick up trash in the churchyard before services began.

Daddy was a gifted guitar player. He could make his guitar sing the very words of any song! People loved to hear him play because he could raise the spirit in a way that people could not help but get up, sing praises to God and shout in spiritual dance. Daddy played his guitar until he was no longer able to, due to his struggle with health issues. He had a history of high blood pressure and had suffered a total of three strokes that left him deaf and eventually bedridden. Despite his health problems, Daddy would always testify, *"The Lord is holding me in the palm of His hand."* As a child, I witnessed Daddy going through his wilderness and I never heard him complain or say, *"Why me, Lord?"* His faith seemed to carry him through the storms of his wilderness.

I am proud to be my Daddy's daughter, but he was only responsible for building half of the strong foundation upon which I would later depend on to keep me stable and strong at critical times. My mother, whom I affectionately call "Mother", built the other half of my foundation. She worked outside of the home when Daddy's illness rendered him disabled. Despite her busy and often hectic schedule, she always paid attention to each of the individual needs of her children. No matter how heavy things were, she had this magical way of making them light. Mother was my first teacher. She taught me how to pray and always be thankful for the smallest things in life. I watched Mother, so full of grace and wisdom, as she navigated her way through the wilderness times in her own life. Mother made sure that all of her children went to school and behaved themselves. Mother would firmly remind us, *"You are a child of God, no matter what! So, behave accordingly."* In being children of God, we were rich in everything. God would have it no other way.

When I left home in 1982, I traveled across the United States, visited several countries and had various experiences along the way. It was not until I began to ask myself questions like: *"Why am I here?"*, *"Where is my voice?"*, *"What is my truth?"* and *"What is my purpose?"* did my life begin to become more meaningful to me. Up until that time, I was like a feather floating through life on a gentle breeze.

In 1996, I moved back to the East Coast from Sacramento, California to be closer to family who were settled in North Carolina. During that time I was working as a computer systems engineer and had accepted a position in Harrisburg, Pennsylvania. Upon moving to Harrisburg, I immediately began to explore my new home, looking for what I could involve myself in, besides work. One day while I was out driving around the city, I came upon this plaza called, Kline Village. As I drove slowly through trying to see the various stores, my eye caught a glimpse of what looked like an African-centered store. My eyes lit up and I immediately looked for a place to park my car. I walked up to the door, just as a middle-aged African American gentleman was at the door, with a key in his hand about to lock up. He must have seen the excitement in my eyes turn to disappointment as I realized that I had gotten there too late. He opened the door for me and cordially greeted me. He said, *"I was about to close, but it's okay, take your time and look around."* Like a lioness, I scanned the entire store and saw wonderful books written by African American authors, African American greeting cards, African clothing and lots of other African-centered trinkets and artifacts. I walked around quickly, in an effort not to keep the store owner waiting. I bought some greeting cards and went to the counter to check out. On the counter was a flyer, advertising an African History study group that met on Wednesday nights there at the store. This sparked my interest, so I asked the nice store owner about the flyer. He told me that the study group would be having its first meeting on that upcoming Wednesday and would be meeting there in the store after closing. I was excited! I thanked him for his generosity and promised to come back to shop some more and to check out the study group.

On that following Wednesday evening, I drove to Kline Village, excited and filled with anticipation of finding out more about this African History study group. I walked in, introduced myself to the people who were sitting in the semi-circle of chairs in the corner of the store. That night, I learned the meaning of the word, *"Sankofa"*, which means - *"We must go back and reclaim our past so we can move forward; so we understand why and how we came to be who we are today."* Learning this somehow had a profound effect on me, creating a stir deep within me. That night marked the beginning of the process of my "re-membering" my purpose for being here.

Over the next few weeks and months, that stir from deep within me became a full blown whipping machine, churning through my entire mind, body, and spirit – waking me up, bringing me into consciousness. I felt new life flowing through my veins, with every book I read, video I watched or lecture I heard from people like Dr. Frances Cress Welsing, Carter G. Woodson, Dr. Jewel Pookrum, Dr. John Henrik Clarke, Dr. Naim Akbar, Dr. Marimba Ani and many others. I began to see with "new eyes" and hear with "new ears". I was being taught about the rich African heritage that I was a direct descendent of. For the first time in my life, I knew - without a doubt, that God had a higher purpose for me. I had a strong desire to "awaken" others, just as I had been awakened.

My wilderness experience began to emerge after I made a commitment to help uplift and awaken my people. I made a career change from being a highly paid computer systems engineer to a low paid Youth Counselor position. Despite that, I was never happier in my life. I knew that now I was living my life "on purpose". I was helping children and it was through my work as a youth counselor that I became aware of the hopelessness, pain, anger, loneliness, rejection and sense of abandonment from a child's perspective. It caused me to reflect on my own life as a child and I began to count my blessings. Later, I gained experience with children in the inner city schools, which was truly an eye opener for me. I realized that I had lived somewhat a sheltered life in comparison to what I was being exposed to from the children I worked with. As a child growing up with my siblings, to say the word, *"fart"* was like cursing, and it would be whispered if said at all. I heard more four-lettered words and swearing than I cared to hear coming from a child. Where was the respect? I realized that, in most cases, it was never taught and what I was witnessing was the anger and disappointment of not being cared for properly. I was then exposed to the fragility of the human mind when I began working with mentally ill adults. Of all of my experiences, I realized that mentally ill people were intriguing to me on one hand and repulsive on the other.

I studied metaphysics and other Gnostic teachings, which seemed to further unfold the universe before me. The more I learned about myself, the more I appreciated and saw the beauty in others. Over a course of about three years, my life had transformed from that of a fuzzy little caterpillar, to a life wrapped in the rich silk of a safe cocoon. I had armored myself with self-knowledge and had established a true connection with my Creator. Deep within the core of my being, I knew that God was preparing me for the work I came into this world to do. I had to go through the wilderness to get to it, though.

In 2004, I embarked on my journey to commit my life to serving people as a spiritual leader. I chose a traditional African spiritual track that was very similar to the religious beliefs that I had grown up in my home and at Mount Livingstone United Holy Church, where the living spirit of God was made manifest in our daily lives. In embracing this traditional African spiritual journey, I realized that I had been taken back to the ancient beliefs of my ancestors – what an honor!

Up to this point it was sunshine and blue skies, when all of a sudden a thunder bolt shot through the sky. Out of nowhere, a mentally ill woman made a threat on my life. Because she was "crazy", I no longer felt safe and became hyper vigilant in my travels, as I didn't know what this woman might try to do. The sky had grown dark in my world and the wind had become stronger. I kept on walking and began to pray, *"The LORD is my shepherd; I shall not want. He maketh me to lie down in green pastures: he leadeth me beside the still waters. He restoreth my soul: he leadeth me in the paths of righteousness for his name's sake. Yea, though I walk through the valley of the shadow of death, I will fear no evil: for thou art with me; thy rod and thy staff they comfort me. Thou preparest a table before me in the presence of mine enemies: thou anointest my head with oil; my cup runneth over. Surely goodness and mercy shall follow me all the days of my life: and I will dwell in the house of the LORD forever."* (Psalms 23) I overcame my fear, for I knew that God was with me. Now, I had never dealt with the legal system before, but I took legal action against that evil "beast" lurking in the wilderness, who was trying to block my path. I kept on walking and before I knew it the wind had shifted and it was now at my back, pushing me further on my journey.

A few months later, my husband was diagnosed with lymphoma (cancer of the lymph nodes) with high probability of it being in the third stage of four. I could feel the winds picking up again… The doctors discussed with us various types of chemotherapy and treatment options. I prayed for him and also asked him to accompany me to the house of worship to receive more prayer. Having grown up in a devout Christian family, I knew the power of prayer and had witnessed many healings. Especially the healings that took place in my father's life when he was going through health challenges. At the worship service, God delivered the message that the doctors were not correct in their diagnosis of my husband and advised on what needed to be done for him.

Later, the oncologist treating my husband referred him to another specialist for a second opinion. The results of the second specialist revealed that my husband "did not" have lymphoma. In fact, the second specialist indicated that he could not believe that my husband was ever diagnosed with the disease. Now, that's God! I was reminded of *Mark 16:18 "… they shall lay hands on the sick, and they shall recover."* I realized that the problem with my husband was only a distraction. Something to throw me off my path, but I used the wind of distraction to further build my faith and trust in God. The whirlwind continued to build in the wilderness, but I was gaining strength with every step I took along the way.

I continued my training as a spiritual leader, traveling to Washington, D.C. every weekend from Harrisburg. In the meantime, two friends and I co-founded a non-profit community-based organization with the mission of *"Promoting education and empowerment for the nurturing and healing of OUR community"*. We were still in the developing stages and had begun to sponsor cultural and educational programs. One spring day, while I was walking along on my journey, a bolt of lightning shot from the sky and a strong wind hit me with a mighty force, nearly knocking me off my feet. My dear friend, who helped co-found our organization, had committed suicide! How could this be…? I felt like the gates of hell had been opened on my life. My friend was a casualty of the whirlwind and storms of his life, suffering a fatal blow. His sudden death made me more determined to accomplish my life's mission. Yes, I was staggered by the force of this whirlwind, but it only propelled me further on my path, with more determination than ever!

I continued my spiritual training, faithfully traveling to Washington, D.C. weekly, despite what was going on in my life. I had made a commitment and I knew that God would see me through. Just as the wind began to calm a little, my husband came home from work one day - I could tell something was wrong as soon as I saw him. We sat down and he began to tell me how he had been unjustly fired from his job. What!!!??? Well, we struggled financially for a while, but being a child of God, I knew He was taking care of everything. So, I was not worried. I filled my mind and heart with thanks and praise for all that we had. There was no room for anything else.

A few months later, after having filed a grievance to shed light on his unjust firing, my husband prevailed and was awarded back pay and all! This whole incident reminded me that there were still "beasts" lurking in the wilderness, trying to block my path by whatever means necessary. As with all the previous storms, it only served to strengthen me on my journey.

One weekend, while I was only a few months from my graduation as an emerging spiritual leader, I traveled to Washington, D.C. as I had done for the previous two years. I parked my car in one of the usual places along the street. However, this day, I decided to lock my purse in the trunk of the car instead of taking it in with me. Later in the day, I needed my purse, so I went out to the car only to find that it was gone!!! I was numb… but I braced myself for the ride on this whirlwind. God is always with me and he always has a *"ram tied in the bush"*. That day, the ram was my dear sister who lived in Maryland, only a few miles away. She made sure I got home safely and handed me a wallet filled with more money than was stolen from me in my car. I filed a police report and in less than a week, my car was found with minimal damages. It's wonderful being a child of God! He has never left me alone or stranded! Again, this whirlwind only served to strengthen me and propel me closer to my mission.

In the spring of 2007, my graduation as a spiritual leader had finally arrived. I had made it through the storms! I emerged from my cocoon sporting my beautiful new butterfly wings and I danced like I had never danced before! The way has been opened for me to help uplift and awaken my people.

The organization that I co-founded with my friends in 2004 is flourishing. We have begun two ongoing programs, one for youth and one for adults. I teach weekly classes that are designed to awaken and increase self-knowledge and empowerment. I am a faculty member of a local chaplains and spiritual leaders institute. God uses me as an instrument to assist with the healing of those who are sent to me. He gave me a Holy Spirit who sits lightly on me, guiding me in all that I do.

The lesson is that there will not always be clear skies and calm winds. God has prepared me with enough armor to overcome anything and anyone who tries to block my path as I tread through the wilderness. I have faith that He will help me ride the whirlwind, whose force serves to propel me further on my way to divinely accomplish any mission. Like the Honorable Marcus Mosiah Garvey once said, *"Look for me in the whirlwind..."*

PRESSING THE MARK

by Toni Emehel

Finding one's purpose in life is wholly about pleasing God. It is more easily discovered than people usually think. It involves three simple steps:

Step One: Get to know Jesus Christ as the way, truth and life (John 14:6). Establishing a personal relationship with Christ is the only way you can please God. This shows *Him* that you have faith in *His* Son, whom *He* sent to die for you so that you might experience eternal life. Many people tend to skip this step when setting course to discover their life's purpose. What they don't realize is that it is impossible to skip to the second step without first completing the first step.

Step Two: After you have developed a personal relationship with Christ, wait on God's timing. If you try to run ahead, God does not feel compelled to bless your endeavors because they are not part of *HIS* plan for you. This is where the faith comes in. If you want God's covering, protection and provision in your life's journey, you must wait on *HIM*.

Step Three: Watch the doors of your dreams begin to open as God calls you out of the crowd as a chosen one to set course on your destiny. *HIS* provision will begin to take reign, working on your behalf to make the unimaginable come true.

PONDERING THOUGHTS

Have you accepted Jesus Christ as your Lord and Savior? If not, say the prayer found in Romans 10:9-10 and watch the miraculous begin to take place in your life as you set course to a life of purpose driven destiny.

Circling the Mountain
by
V. Arleen

CIRCLING THE MOUNTAIN

"It is for this reason, I bow my knees and pray to the Father." --Ephesians 3:14

Even as I pen these words I am in the midst of what seems to be yet another failing relationship. It has gotten to a place where to count anymore is more painful than I can state. Each man was a professed Christian (except the very first one), yet I was betrayed by them all.

"Father, I kneel before You in the holy name of Jesus asking:

When, Father, will enough be enough for me? What are You thinking to call me to this national ministry, for relationships in the body of Christ, even as I feel like the poster child for failed relationships? What are You trying to work in me, Lord, that I don't yet understand? I know enough about You to know that You are working something for my good and for Your glory.

You have a track record with me of always being faithful. So I have no doubt that You are trying to reveal something to me and through me. What lessons have You taken upon Yourself to teach me as it pertains to self and the motivations behind my choices in men? When will this wound heal and stop being opened up a fresh? What have I missed, said, done and/or refused to receive or release that keeps me circling this mountain?

How have I sinned against You? I know that the enemy has no power to stop what You have for me. I know that You are not a man that You should lie. So the error has to be in me. Marriage was instituted and ordained by You so my desire for a husband who loves me according to Your word is according to Your will. Why has this desire gone unfulfilled in my life?

You have given me just about everything else that I have asked You for, even blessings that I didn't ask for. Why have You withheld Your blessing from me in this one thing? You blessed my ex-husband with a beautiful new wife (his third) after he spent the 5 years of our marriage abusing me. Although I prayed for his happiness, his health (mind, body, soul and spirit), and I am truly happy for him, I am a bit confused as to what it is that moved You on his behalf but not mine. Was it my prayers that moved you to bless him as in the case of Moses' prayers for Miriam and Job's prayers for his "friends?"

My marriage, the greatest disappointment of them all, is also the relationship I least regret. I dare say that I don't regret it at all. It was the one relationship that was honorable in Your sight. The lessons were far too valuable to regret. At least he was willing to marry me. Although he only seemed to be looking for a slave, he did put me in a house. He did work everyday and attend church faithfully. He was a faithful tither and a worship leader in the church. I finally seal the deal and still fail. What a blow.

To see a relationship with what I thought was such potential only to find that my little bitty love was actually not enough to heal his pain. How was I to know that my love wasn't enough to cast out his demons? I knew nothing of spiritual warfare. I thought love cured every ill. If only he had been willing to accept it. Outside he was the model husband. Women were asking if he had a brother. Behind closed doors he was like Pharaoh was to the Israelites before their deliverance from Egypt.

The abuse became more than I could stand. I remember the day, only a few months into our marriage when I got a large ceramic bowl of pasta thrown at my head because I wanted to eat at the kitchen table instead of in front of the television as we had done every night since we married. It was by your grace that the bowl missed my head and hit the wall instead. I remember the time he threatened to cut his wrists with a knife. It must have been You who gave me the strength to wrestle his 6'2", 325+ pound frame to the ground and take the knife. I remember the miscarriage after a big argument only a week after finding out that I was expecting our first child. I remember going to an elder and his wife for help for her to tell me that he was only doing this because he loved me and he was trying to get my attention. As if his fits of rage was normal behavior for a 33-year-old man. This was just a few of the things that took place in the first year.

There was no one willing to hold him accountable for his actions. It was all up to me to pray and adapt. There was no regard given to my mental, emotional or spiritual well being in the midst of the abuse even after I finally took him before the Bishop in the last year. It was so painful and frightening to realize that I had no one in my church who would protect me or do anything until after he had done serious harm to me. When he yelled out "God, help me before I hurt her," I knew then that it was time for me to protect myself. There is a scripture that says that a husband should spend the first year of marriage making his new wife happy. He spent the first year instilling fear, intimidation and manipulation into my heart instead. I stayed, not because I needed him, I knew You would take care of me. I had a loving family to turn to. I stayed because I thought he needed me. He had already shown me that he was capable of hurting himself if he was not happy. He had no close family living and this would be his second divorce. I left only after fasting and praying for 40 days. Once You told me that he was never my husband and not Your choice for me, I knew that I must go. You also told me that if I left You would be with me but if I stayed I would have to continue to live with the abuse. I knew that he was killing me from the inside out and I didn't want to die. I wanted to live.

The trauma of separation and divorce was like the pain and shock of being torn asunder by a train, with muscle, tissue, vessels and arteries left exposed and bleeding. He was saved, sanctified and filled with the Holy Spirit. How was I to know that you can be unevenly yoked even in the Body of Christ? How was I to know that I needed to understand what part of the Body I was before I connected to another part to ensure proper connection?

How was I to know that my improper connection could deform the Body and result in a surgical removal to correct the deformity? No one told me these things.

I didn't ask You enough questions before making that connection or the others for that matter. You told me before hand that there were childhood traumas in his life. Me and my big mouth, "Oh I can handle it, Lord. A little TLC will take right good care of that and I am brimming over with it." After the fact, I prayed. I fasted. I cried out for help to no avail. I did all I knew to do. I felt as if I had hurt and failed You both even as I was hurting immeasurably. I didn't want to fail either of You, Father.

I know the abuse is a burden that he must bear on his own shoulders. I just thought that I could hold him up until he got better. I didn't realize how wounded I still was from my own past relationships. Boy did the enemy have a field day with this one. When will Your mercy be towards me? Where will I have to go to have my desires met?

Will I have to get a much older man to find what I need spiritually and emotionally? I don't want to relive my mother's life, Lord. After my father's death when I was eight, she married my stepdad who is 30 years older than she. She felt that this was what she had to do to have a husband who met her needs and it has worked for her.

I know that my Dad met my mother's needs, Father. I am grateful for the environment that she and my Dad were able to give my siblings and me. I felt secure and well loved and cared for to the extent that I thought that we were wealthy. For many years I admired her life so much that I wanted to emulate her in my own life. But I am not my Mother. My needs and desires are not the same as hers. Her ministry was not the same as mine. She already had children and she was content to have a mate who shared her beliefs and loved and cared financially for her and her children. I have yet to experience the wonders of motherhood. Please tell me that I don't have to imitate my mother's life.

I realize that it was Your presence that sustained us all. I also realize that You desire to take us from glory to glory. I want to receive the next level of glory that You have for me. I don't want to covet someone else's blessings, even if that someone is my Mother. I know that You have something and someone just for me. I realize that there are generational curses that have been passed down from my ancestors that need to be destroyed in my own life. I renounce spirits of haughtiness, error and control that are results of religious teachings that were not in line with your Word. I renounce spirits of anxiety, worry and fear that come as a result of not having security and needs met in early years and environments full of strife. I pray Father that You would replace them with spirits of liberty, humility, love, peace, self-control, truth and every spirit that pertains to Your Holy Spirit.

Where is he, Father? Where is that man who will love me as Christ loved the church and gave Himself for it? I feel sick within myself at the waiting. I question my judgment and my ability to make sound decisions. I feel more like a lost child not knowing which direction to go. I don't want to wander anymore. I need You to end this torture for my sake. Open my eyes of understanding. Reveal to me my own error, my own sin. How have I offended You? The exhaustion I feel is almost unbearable, and I am holding on to my convictions with everything that is within me. Hoping beyond hope that You are going to rescue me at any moment now.

How can I know Your righteous, holy and majestic ways? Your ways are not my ways and Your thoughts are not my thoughts. Am I looking for Your will in my life or am I putting other things before You? Can I stand fast even in the midst of the storm? Am I being honest with myself? Father, touch this pain in my soul.

Father, I've heard it said that one shouldn't ask what is wrong with me but in all of these failed relationships I am the common factor. All of the guys were different in many ways. I have been relentless in pursuing the maintenance of these relationships although they have not been able, ready or willing to meet my needs. I entered every one with the mind set of how I could be a blessing to them instead of how they could bless me. So I ask in bewilderment what am I doing wrong? Is it my choices? Is it my attitude? Am I settling for less and thus getting less? What is it?

As it is written in the book of Matthew 7:6-8 I am earnestly and honestly seeking answers that seem to keep alluding me. I don't want to live my life in perpetual relationship failure, pain and turmoil. Father, have mercy on me! Could it be that I am asking for something for which I am not yet prepared? Could my own fears be getting the best of me? Could it be that I yet need healing? What harm have I done to myself over the years with ungodly soul ties, my choices of music, media and literature?

Is it possible that my steady, daily diet of romance novels, love songs, television and movies as a young girl may have created much of the dis-ease that I am experiencing? Could this diet have distorted my view of relationships and caused a subtle dysfunction that I was unaware of? Is that why you moved on my spirit to completely give up the music and books when I converted? Will You undo the damage that has been done? Set me free from the fear of being alone.

Admit me into Your hospital for further care and observation so that I do not reinjure myself as I heal. Put me in the capable hands of Your Holy Spirit for the nursing comfort that I need at this time in my life. I don't want to pass this dis-ease on to my children. I willfully lay upon Your cold steel surgical table and allow You to take Your scalpel to this wound and cut out anything that would prevent it from healing properly once and for all. Remove scar tissue and dead cells. Clean out infection and puss. Stop the bleeding, Father. Sow up vessels and arteries that have been severed. Transfuse me with the blood of Jesus. Sew up the layers of skin; treat and bandage my wounds so that they may properly heal.

Help me to forget those things which are behind, the pain, the betrayals and the disappointments, so that I can trust in You and get back my faith. Father, I need confidence in my own happiness and joy in my own life. I need and want to believe You for my own blessings and the desires of my own heart. I don't want fear and doubt to steal my chance at the abundant life that I encourage others about. Father, I need You to intervene on my behalf and help my unbelief. I need You to calm my fears. I need You to override my emotions and my memory. Override the memory of too many failures.

Give me back that innocent hope, faith and love that used to be such an enormous part of my life. I want it back, Father. I need You to make up the difference for what I don't know and don't understand. I need You to carry me over the hurdles that I can not jump. Restore the joy of my salvation and renew a right spirit in me. "I cannot"-"I will not" die in the wilderness.

This is my petition to you, on this day. Thank you for hearing my prayer and delivering me from all my troubles. I am Your child, in need of answers, in need of your blessing.

In Jesus name I pray --Amen."

Albeit painful, I have to share this with you, because as I share it I receive healing to my inner self. I remind myself of God's presence with me and I get the benefits of overcoming by the blood of the Lamb and the word of my testimony. I'm still here! The enemy has not succeeded in taking me out! To God be the Glory!

I have known much pain, but each time I feel the presence of God with me greater than the time before. Let me share with you the lessons that I have learned in the midst of my pain:

- Let go, forgive and pray for the men and let God do the rest. Many of them were in their own wilderness and using whomever they could to mask their own pain and confusion. Just like the Israelites, not everyone makes it out of the wilderness alive.

- Look for what has been gained from the experience instead of looking at what was lost. There is a lesson for you in every experience you go through.

- It is of utmost importance to ask the right questions not just of God but of men as well. If a man does not want to answer questions it is a red flag.

- It is dangerous and unhealthy for the body, soul and spirit to stay in a relationship that is abusive in any way and where an individual is not ready, willing and/or able to meet my needs as well as me meeting theirs.

- Each person is responsible for their own choices. If one chooses death over life that is their right. I also know that it is my right to choose not to die with them or by their hands. Christ died for my sins and the sins of men because I can not and so that I would not have to.

Today I know that just as God promised that the Israelites would never see Pharaoh and his army again just before He closed the waters of the Red Sea on them, I will not have to see this pain ever again (Ex.14:13,14). It is finished. It is time to walk in the ministry and abundance that Jesus came, lived and died that I might walk in (John10:10). Because of this I can boldly profess that I am the righteousness of God (2Cor.5:21).

This is my wilderness experience. For some of you who may not know what a wilderness experience is: It is a place where you have just enough to make it through each day, just enough spiritually and/or naturally. It is a place of great challenge and much testing and trying of your faith. It is a transitional place that, if you can keep your faith in God, leads to a Land of More Than Enough. This place is the place where you are blessed to be a blessing. The wilderness experience can be an instrument for multiple uses. It can be a place where we find out where our hearts are as in the case of the Israelites (Deut.8:1-3). It can be a place of escape as in Hagar's case (Gen.16:6-9). It can be a platform for ministry as in the case of John the Baptist. It can also be the place where we prepare for our ministry calling as was the case with Jesus (Lu. 5:16) Thank God that He always knows where you are. He can and will find, lead and deliver you from the wilderness in His own time. What is the purpose of your wilderness experience?

This is where you take time to go to God in prayer for it is only He who holds the answer to this question. Don't lose heart and don't lose faith (Lu.18:1). Make the most of your wilderness experience. Your attitude in the wilderness is an important factor in how your experience ends. Don't, like the Israelites, let the wrong attitude take the blessings that God has for you on the other side of your wilderness experience (Num.14:20-38; Josh.5:6; Heb.3:16-18). The wilderness is the perfect place to learn more about yourself, God and His will for your life. It is also a great place to draw closer to Him and mature in your walk with Him. Be determined to make it to the Promised Land. Let your declaration be as mine, "I Shall Not Die in the Wilderness!"

Before I close, I would like to thank God for the mother who set a godly example and loves me in spite of all my bad decisions and wrong choices. To the sisters who looked upon me as a woman of God and lent emotional support and love in my time of brokenness, I thank you. For the spiritual mother whose sweet spirit was always there to encourage me, I thank you. For the accountability partner who helped me not to give up and to refocus my eyes on You, I thank you. For the friend with whom I could laugh at myself, confess, share, pray and cry without shame, guilt or condemnation, I thank you. For the Angel that You sent to minister to me during my divorce. Thank You for the mentor who came in and helped me make the transition from uncertain little girl into a woman of prayer, purpose and power. Every woman should have such a blessed arsenal of women. Thank you for the courage to reach out to them for help instead of letting the enemy trick me into thinking that I am all alone. Thank you for the men and women of God who ministered to me from a distance through the preached word and song. These men and women who have no clue how they were being used by you for my benefit preached or sung a word of confirmation, revelation and restoration. Some sung my very heart and soul to glory. Some I used to speak for me. Even with all these there are some things that go so deep that only You can get to without doing permanent damage.

As I look back on all of those relationships I realize that God was not keeping anything good from me instead He was protecting the gifts and anointing which He has placed on my life. He was trying to show me my relationship with Him. While I was willing to be in a relationship with Him, I was not willing to fully commit to His will for my life. God wanted better for me although I was willing to settle. Every severed connection was for my good. He is deliberately keeping me from making connections to anyone who could potentially cause me to abort my destiny. My own persistence in pursuing someone over my pursuit of His will has put me off track and behind repeatedly. God is yet faithful and He is determined to get a return on the investment that He has made in me.

I now understand that God is building my testimony. The word says we overcome by the blood of the lamb and the word of our testimony. Because of what I have been through there are a number of women, both young and old, that will not have to go through what I have been through. As I share my testimony and the lessons that God taught me someone will learn from it and be set free from the deception of the enemy.

Look for my upcoming book entitled, "The Lies the Enemy Told Me" (to be published yearend 2009) as I go deeper into the lies that the enemy tells us (like he did Eve in the Garden of Eden) and how giving in to those lies affects our relationships with God and others. It will also reveal God's ammunition for quenching the fiery darts of the enemy and how to use them.

I also welcome you to join us on the Restoring Relationships in the Body of Christ prayer/discussion conference line. You may send me an email at: RestoringRelationshipsInTheBOC@yahoo.com to be added to the mailing list for more information.

PRESSING THE MARK

by Toni Emehel

How long will you circle the mountain of life looking toward another to fill the God-shaped void placed within you? God wants us to realize that we will never be able to freely move into a genuine relationship with another person until we realize that the emptied cisterns embedded within us need to be filled with *HIM*. In our quest to be relational, the moment we find satisfaction in the filling of *HIS* cistern by the antics of another being, that being becomes a false god in our lives. Then we begin to look toward that being as our source of life, love, protection and happiness.

There is nothing wrong with desiring to be in an intimate relationship. God intended for us to be relational beings with a natural desire for companionship and intimacy. However, *HE* never intended for these natural desires to replace our desire for *HIM*.

PONDERING THOUGHTS

To whom are you looking to as your source of love, life, joy, peace, happiness and protection? Read Psalms 118:8 and allow God to speak to your heart. If your response was anything other than God, pray for a divine revelation of *His Word* and a filling of the Holy Spirit to guide you.

However, through His word, God corrected me.
—Janie F. Edmond-Reid

Youch! I'm Stuck in a Briar Patch

by

Janie F. Edmond-Reid

YOUCH! I'M STUCK IN A BRIAR PATCH

"Happy is the man that findeth wisdom, and the man that getteth understanding."

—*Proverbs 3:13*

Some people say I should have thrown in the towel years ago. I guess I'm a glutton for punishment or maybe it's simply because I truly love this thorn God has lodged in my flesh. At times, when it feels like I am rolling around in a briar patch, I wonder if this is the same man I married. Then, when I think back on all the things I saw in him then, I have to be honest with myself and say, *"Yes, it's the same man I found in the briar patch of life, way back then."* He had prickles on him then, as did I. Only now, those prickles have now been lodged in my side. Because of that, I live each day to escape the prickly briar patch of my wilderness, which is shaped by self-centeredness, lack and shame.

I keep trying to figure out where I went wrong. Had I not married the love of my youth? He knows of the good bloodline I came from. We dated when we were teens. He knew my family and I knew his. Though I went off to the military after high school, we still found our way back to each other and eventually married. Surely, this is the man that God would have me to spend the rest of my life with, but Lord, please NOT LIKE THIS!

There is no question about it, I'm hurting right now. God has me in a holding pattern like no other experience in my life. What is clear to me is that He has me in this position to show me some things. I firmly believe that I am in this wilderness to come to terms with myself, discover the dept of my true relationship with God, and draw my husband to Christ.

I have been in this wilderness for a little more than eight years now, and I keep wondering how much longer God will keep me in this maze. Perhaps, if I begin to share those things I have learned in the wilderness, God will favor me and part the trees so that I may escape. I have come to understand that God does not give us experiences like these to keep only to ourselves, but to share with others so that they too may learn of His grace and restorative power. So, what you are about to read is a testament of my faith, growth and restoration. Beginning with these three thoughts:

1. I was so caught up in feeling loved, that I did not anticipate the cultural differences stemming from the different upbringings my husband and I experienced as children. I came from a Christian upbringing and he didn't. The bible would call this being unequally yoked, but I never saw us that way. Now, don't get me wrong. Even though my husband did not come from a Christian home, he came from a good home.

2. I went into my marriage with the 50/50 expectation, honestly expecting that my husband would meet me halfway in ALL things. I never anticipated the pain resulting from unmet expectations.

3. I failed to realize the importance of my husband having a personal relationship with Jesus Christ, before we got married. So how can Christ truly be the head of my home?

Where to start…WHERE TO START seems to be the question for me. I have always thought of myself as "simple", but this is a "complex" issue that I have to deal with here. I don't ask for a lot and typically don't expect a lot. Now, I'm beginning to think I expect too much. You see, I am what some would call, *"a good ole' country girl"* at heart. I get simple pleasures out of the little things. Like running through cornfields, climbing apple trees to shake the limbs in order to make the ripened apples fall, or even running down a back country dirt road to trek on a beaten path leading to blackberry patches where my siblings and I would pick blackberries year after year after year. I came from the land of good and plenty. My parents always kept a garden where they raised corn, cabbage, snap bean, butter beans, rutabagas and turnips. If it wasn't grown in the garden, nature provided it for us in the natural growth of the many fruit trees that grew in the wild growth bordering the farm we lived on.

I attribute this to the relationship that both my mother and father had with Christ. My Father helped build the church we attended in Selma, North Carolina and served as a Deacon on their board. While my Mother served as an evangelist missionary. So, needless to say, my family was rich in God's blessings, even though most would look on us and think we were poor. Being the ninth of 10 children, I can firmly say that God always supplied our needs, wants and more. I never felt lack of anything. To top it all off, we were a family rich in love. There were very few arguments and bickering amongst siblings and I can not recall a time where my parents ever engaged in an argument in my presence. So, as you can see, the thorn I'm dealing with now is of a foreign nature to me.

Please understand that while I refer to my husband as the thorn divinely placed in my flesh, he is simply a conduit God used to draw me nearer to Him. My husband is a good man. He's got some issues…and I do too! But, there ain't no reason why I have to bring home the bacon, fry it up in a pan *(like the Enjole perfume commercial)*, cut the grass, wax the floors and care for the kids too! Oh, and don't forget making him feel like a man! I'm not complaining…Oh yes I am and I'm sure my husband has some complaints about me too. But this is my story.

The fact of the matter is that, there are some things in him that his mother should have beat out of him as a boy. Things like *"laziness"*, *"unproductiveness"*, the *"get something for nothing"* spirit. I imagine if he were writing this story, his story might read… *"instead of her mother trying to raise a STRONG black woman, she should have raised a woman who would knows her place in the home and how to submit to her man."* And to that, I would say, *"submit to what?"* A gal's got to know what she is submitting to. Get yourself a vision and then maybe I'll submit.

Do y'all see what I'm dealing with here? Lord knows I love my husband, but I don't think either of us really knew what we were getting into when we got married. I believe we were still hanging on to the reigns of the puppy love we shared as teenagers. My husband and I met when I was 16 years old. We were both very young and thought that love had all to do with that warm fuzzy feeling one gets from knowing their true love is just a doors knock away. Back then, we were perfect for each other. We shared some of the same character traits; quiet, soft spoken, not easily angered. He seemed to embrace some of the same core values that my parents had instilled in me.

Even then, the handwriting was on the wall. I just couldn't see it. A typical date for us was McDonalds and a movie. Don't laugh! It was the 1980's and we were just in high school. You were eating good, if you got your boyfriend to take you to McDonalds. Only, when my boyfriend took me, I almost always had to share some of the tab. Not to mention, pitching in two or three dollars for gas. Keep in mind, that gas was about 39 cents a gallon during that time. So, my two or three dollars would get him about a half tank of gas in that big red Ford Torino he used to drive.

I didn't think nothing of it back then. Now, here I am some 20 plus years later; still chipping in for dinner when we go out to eat, footing the entire bill to keep food on our table, and every now and again…fronting 50 to 60 dollars for gas to keep his Dodge Ram pick up truck filled. Man, oh man…where did I go wrong? I used to hear folks say, *"Marriage without finance equals to no romance."* Little did I know that cliché would come to my door steps to roost. The thing that keeps running through my mind is that this was not supposed to happen to us. My husband and I were each other's backbone.

Let me tell you this; after jumping that broomstick of marriage, I have seen a whole new side of romancing and financing. These are some things I would have done differently:

1. I would have gotten to know my husband's family a little better. Particularly, the men who shaped his life. Were these men strong, God-fearing men who believed in providing for their families? What kind of examples did they set for him? Did they believe that a man should be the head of his home in all things, particularly finances? I could have been spared a lot of sleepless nights, if I had just taken the time to get to know a little bit more about my husband's upbringing.

2. I would have asked my husband the tough question, "Do you have a personal relationship with God?"

   The reason I would have asked this question is because a man who does not have a relationship with God usually cares more about himself than he does anyone else. A man without Christ is out for himself. He will put you in a position of compromising your relationship with God for his own gain. Prime example, co-signing for a car; a man without Christ in his life don't mind messing up his credit and yours too if it will get him what he wants.

A man without Christ in his life does not place a value on church and don't believe in submitting to another man, much less a woman. He is a man of NO accountability and can't be told NOTHING *(pardon my slang, but I feel my hometown rising up in me)*.

3. I should have learned his expectations, while telling him mine. Perhaps we should have gone through some Christian premarital classes to help us transition from a dating couple to a married couple with a plan. If we had gone through that process, we would have been compelled to count up the cost of becoming a family. Maybe, I would have learned that a man without a vision is destined for failure. Plainly put, without a vision, how can any man lead his home without a vision? Where is he leading them? If I had an understanding of this concept before I got married, my husband could have set our house in order from the start. Instead, here we are some eight years later, rolling around in our marital thicket, pricking and gauging each other every chance we get.

They say, *"Hindsight is 20/20"*. I tend to disagree. It ain't 20/20 until you have learned to analyze life situations, interpret the information you've received from it and begin to respond to what you have seen in confidence. Well, my sight ain't 20/20 yet, but it's getting there. That husband of mine...I declare, he is just legally blind! No matter how much I hoop and holler about our situation, he just sits there like a bump on a log saying, *"What?"* Like he don't know the bills need to be paid and the kids got to eat. I never knew that a man could adequately support his family by sleeping in and taking days off work just to sit around the house like a piece of furniture, in my way. If I had gotten to know his family a little better, hung around his mother's house just a little longer, I would have known that he does not know the value of a keeping a JOB.

Don't get me wrong, I am not a gold-digger, but I do believe a man who is married with children needs to pull his weight. Even if he cannot get a job because of the economy, there are a lot of other things that he could do to make up for his lack of gainful employment. He could fix things around the house, get the cars maintenance, rake the leaves in the front yard or even cut the grass. There is *SOMETHING* he can do, besides wearing out the leather on my couch, to partner with the helpmate who has been faithfully carrying his weight. I want to say to my husband, *"Look at me. I'm a woman. God didn't design me to be the moneymaker, honey taker, and yard raker too!"* But, we all know how that would go over…in one ear and out the other.

I now realize that my current situation could have been avoided if God was the first order of business in my marriage. My Mother has always told me that, *"Without a vision people will perish."* Nothing strange about it, I've heard it all my life and it came straight out of the bible (Proverbs 29:18). After being through all I've been through with this man of mine, I truly know what the scripture means! I am bleeding dry with a God-given thorn in my side who does not know who he is in God. Consequently, he does not relish me as God commands him to, as my husband. The word of God says that, men should love their wives as they love themselves. All I want to say is, *"Where's the love?"*

I realize I'm writing this story in a comedic manner, and may have exaggerated some issues just to make a point. But these issues are real and they lurk in many households throughout the country. If you have these same or similar issues in your home, take my advice: you need to pray about developing a plan for your marriage. This will be the lubricant that keeps the wheels of your relationship from falling off. In order to do this, you must start with prayer. Begin to seek God's perfect will for your marriage. When I did this, the Holy Spirit directed me to the center of God's word; Psalms 118:8, which told me, *"It is better to trust in the Lord than to put my confidence in man."*

WOW, that took me for a loop! Sounded like to me, *(my hometown lingo again)* that God was letting my husband off the hook. How could I take my eyes off him? In my mind, my husband was at the crux of the pain and discomfort in our marriage. Accordingly, I felt like all my attention should be on him and getting him to change his ways. However, through *His* word, God corrected me. I was lead to realize that if I wanted to be in the center of God's will for my marriage, I had to take my eyes off my husband and focus them on God. Once I turned my focus to God, I realized that the only one that can change my husband is God. For that matter, the only one that can change me is God. I found that all I needed to do to strengthen my marriage was to seek a closer relationship with God and everything else would fall in place. Well ya'll, I'm still seeking and I ain't ashamed to say it. To try and make you think anything different would be prideful on my part.

Outside of God, my husband is the love of my life! For me there is no other. Though we wrestle in the briar patch from time to time, that man of mine can still put a twinkle in my eye when he enters in a room. After we remove the thorns we've lodged into each others flesh from life's struggles and complacency, we still take time to shop for scented candles and incense to brighten our scene of romance. There is a plan for my marriage, and that plan is Christ Jesus. For with HIM, together my husband and I shall find our joy, peace and happiness.

PRESSING THE MARK
by Toni Emehel

When God created marriage, *HE* intended for it to be more than a natural progression through life. More and more couples are carelessly entering the institution of marriage without defining the functional roles of the husband and wife. Consequently, God's intended purpose for marriage is not being met by many married couples today. This is evident by national divorce rates.

In order to meet God's expectation for marriage, husbands and wives need to sanctify each other through the work of *HIS* grace. This means that each is to inspire the other to live a life of holiness by first setting an example of holiness in their own lives. Both husband and wife have a responsibility to assist the other in sanctification. This can not happen if neither or the other does not have a biblical mission in God.

PONDERING THOUGHTS

There is a biblical proverb that says:

Marry a Man without a biblical mission and you will have no eternal vision; Marry a Man without his eternal vision and you will violate your biblical mission!

Marry a Woman who does not believe in the biblical mission and you will lose your vision; Marry a Woman who does not have the biblical vision and you will fail at your eternal mission!

What does this mean to you? And how does the above proverb apply to your current life situation?

It is human nature to feel a need to belong.
—Tina L. Massey

The Pain behind the Mask

by

Tina L. Massey

THE PAIN BEHIND THE MASK

I am your father and I love you even as I love my son…

—John 17:23

Admittedly, there have been times in my life when I have gladly accepted the gruesome hand of abuse, rejection and defeat over the dim cloud of loneliness that dominated my existence. The struggles of life were a daily battle for me during this period, but it was something that I had to go through to realize God's love for me. The truth is, deep down I was convinced that no one really cared about me or my feelings.

Have you ever felt that way? Have you ever felt like you were an invisible outsider, viewing the world through the panes of a dark fogged window? Have you ever felt like you have been overlooked by everyone around you, last to none and the world just did not understand you? People in your life picking on you because you don't look like they look; talk like they talk or have the same swing in your hair that they do? Have you ever experienced being called every name in the book, except a child of God? Have you ever experienced being laughed at, scorned or ridiculed for being the only person you know how to be?

Pretty soon, you begin to believe that the world has nothing to offer you, but a bad deal. You began to retreat within yourself and become your only best friend. You begin to feel like anyone who tries to befriend you is after something. They just want to use and abuse you; make you feel like you don't have any other choice but to allow them to have their way with you. Pretty soon, you yourself begin to welcome the use and abuse because you are lonely…just plain ole lonely.

Loneliness is a powerful feeling of emptiness that supersedes the presence of people around you. My state of loneliness sat in as a young child. I use to hear people say, *"stick and stones may break your bones but words will never hurt you,"* I beg to differ. It was the words of people that literally tore me apart inwardly, as I began to mask the pain of rejection and fear of not being accepted for who I was. After a while, I began to wonder if anyone noticed how I really felt about what they were saying about me or if they even cared that being the object of their fun and laughter hurt me. When you are in a situation like that, you begin to feel worthless. I felt abandoned. In fact, I would stand in the mirror and chastise myself because I felt as if my being mistreated by the world was entirely my fault. If you have ever walked in these shoes, then you realize that depression soon sets in. Following the onset of depression in my life, I loss my desire to live. I began to tell myself, "enough is enough, I'm checking out and I'm throwing in the towel." Can we be transparent just for a moment? What I want to know is, am I on your trail? Am I describing your innermost feelings that only you and God share? Well if I am, you are in the right chapter.

My journey in the wilderness of loneliness and fear caused me to realize that struggles come in many forms. While some people struggle through sickness, others may struggle through a divorce, loss of a loved one, abuse, rejection and financial distress. Whatever the struggle, we find that some people may go through it alone and in silence for various reasons. Some of the reasons could be that they feel they will be criticized by society or it could be because they feel they can never measure up to society's expectations. For these reasons they stand alone in life and debate whether they want to live with those aggravating struggles and thoughts of feeling alone in this world or simply lie down and die.

Some people have grown up with a prophecy placed over their heads by another that they will never be anything. They are doomed from anything good happening to them in their lifetime. Just like *Celie*, in the movie, *"The Color Purple"*, there are some people who have been told by others that they are on a journey to nowhere unless that person is a part of their life. When you looked at where you came from and where you are headed, it seems that the other person may be telling the truth.

It is an awkward and degrading feeling to believe you have to succeed through the shadow of another person; especially, a person who hurts you. It is a scary and lonely road you feel you must travel in silence, all by yourself.   As people often say, *"I've been there…done that,"* and believe me, I have got the battle scars to show it.

I began suffering wounds of my journey in a small rural town located in the eastern part of North Carolina. This was a town where most everyone knew each other. All you had to say was your last name and people could associate you with at least one of your relatives. Because the town was so small, our family name carried its share of weight and value. If success, trouble, illness or death occurred, everybody in town knew about it by the end of the day. It didn't take long for town gossip to spread. Whose child it was that succeeded in what, who committed what crime, who got ill, or died, you name it, and within a day news would have traveled throughout the town.

People in our town could even associate your last name with former playmates or classmates that grew up in the same time period as you did. One of the good things about this small town was that most everything and everyone were within walking distance. The town contained one elementary school, one junior high school and one high school. No matter where you lived, as long as it was in town limits, you attended one of those schools. All the churches were small enough that you knew who was there on a particular Sunday and who was not.

Being a product of a religious family, it was expected that children go to church every Sunday. If my siblings or I got up on Sunday morning and were not deathly ill, and told our parents that we did not feel like going to church, they would say, *"if you are sick church is the best place for you,"* and off to church we were sent. My parents were active members at what we called "the family church", which was located in a neighboring city. My siblings and I were active members of a church that was within walking distance of our home.

My siblings and I got along with the children in the neighborhood we lived in, but we, like other children, often had our differences that sometimes led to arguing, fussing and…even fighting. My siblings and I were all taught not to fight. Yet, each time one of the neighborhood children would start an argument with me and my mother found out, she would always call me to the carpet and make me apologize to the child whom she knew started the argument. She was teaching me to love those I would rather hate. My mother often told me that there would be a *"star on my crown"* and that *"my actions would heap coals of fire on their head"*. Though I didn't really know what that meant as a child, I now realize that she was referring to the scripture, Romans 12:17-21, where the Apostle Paul expounds on how to respond to people who treat you badly. Basically, my mother was trying to teach me how to live in peace with other people while letting God avenge the wrongs that people had committed against me.

Being the obedient child I was, I would always apologize, but it did little for my image or my ego because, as a result, the other kids laughed at me; continued to pick on me and I was thought of as being afraid of my rival. Deep down on the inside, it was a hurtful feeling. I felt like I was all alone as the other children sided with the one they thought was more victorious in the fight. So much for living in peace, which is what everyone else seemed to have…just not me? So, I retreated within myself and found a friend I could count on.

At the age of eight, I started playing the piano. Music was my best friend, my passion and my hiding place. I dreamed of becoming a concert pianist. I played a variety of music, but my favorite was classical. Classical music took me to an unimaginable level of comfort zones, because it allowed me to dismiss how I was feelings inwardly as I played through the loneliness and rejection to enter into a different world. I did not have to open my mouth to talk to anyone, if I chose not to do so. I found a way to communicate through my music, in such a manner that people could not see my pain. Although my parents and others felt I was just playing a nice tune, they did not know I was playing outside of myself or how I was really feeling on the inside. But that was my intended purpose, because this was the time I had to steal away and be silent and not worry about the world or how I felt I was being treated in it. Sometimes as I played there was either an immediate family member or a crowd around me listening in awe. It was the only thing I felt people enjoyed about me.

During my middle school years, I never had any friends that uplifted me; instead I was the laughing stock of the flock, if I was around because I was overweight, had short hair and was not among the elite smart kids. I often laughed at myself to withstand the pain of everyone else laughing at me, including some of the teachers. My mother was one that would sometimes know when something was wrong with me. Each time she asked me what was wrong and when I told her, she would give me the same response, *"just pray."* Instead, I would just play a tune on the piano to describe my pain without outwardly speaking how I really felt at that moment. I often asked myself the question, *"were people back then too religious to expose wrongdoers for the wrongs they had done? Or was it truly their strong faith and belief that God avenges all wrongs done against His people?"*

Around the age of thirteen, my older brother, the one person I could relate to was killed. When I heard the news, I could not believe it. People from all over town came to my house to mourn his death, but I stayed to myself in my room with a closed door. I felt I was alone and I wanted to be, because I did not want people to watch me as I mourned. I was scared that they would just laugh at me like they always did, so I mourned in silence. Shortly after my brother's funeral, my mother remembered that she never saw me cry. She asked me why? I did not have an answer to give her. I only hoped that she knew that I cried within my heart, for my heart was drenched with tears that she could not see. I just looked at her, smiled and walked away to my room, as I felt the emerging tears well up in my eyes. When I got to the private chambers of my room, I turned up the volume on my stereo and there in my pillow a river of tears flowed as I released the pain that was buried deep inside me.

Though he was my brother, he was my closest friend. He accepted me for who I was, didn't care how I looked and understood the pain I was going through. Without my brother in my life the loneliness I experienced began to fill an even bigger place in my life. My best friend was gone and all the neighborhood children (who I wouldn't necessarily call friends, rather playmates) were getting involved in other interests, sports, dating and such, I was all by myself. The thing about loneliness is that, it can sometimes disposition you for tragic situations you never imagined you would encounter in your lifetime. Loneliness can cause a person to enter into counterfeit relationships and become deceived by harmful intentions and false motives of those not having our best interest in mind.

Unfortunately, I learned this the hard way at the innocent age of 14. Out of my loneliness, I embraced the friendship of a school mate, only to later be beaten and raped by him while returning home from church one Sunday afternoon. I had never encountered such a traumatic experience, neither had I ever been with a man sexually. After a long and humiliating walk down the country roads of our homespun town with blood on my clothes, I arrived home emotionally devastated with grief, overwhelmed with fear and drenched in my tears. There was no one there to greet me, so I used this time to cleanse the bloody shame from my body and gather my thoughts before my parents would arrive home.

Embarrassed by the incident, I isolated the pain because I did not want them to know of the violent act that had ruined my virginity. I feared what my parents would think. My inner questions were who would they blame? Would I be told to remain silent to protect the family name? When my parents arrived home, I was in my room. My mother opened my door to look in on me and I greeted her as if nothing had happened. But deep down inside me, I was hurting agitated with fear and shame because I had been robbed of my innocence. As a result, I became even more distrustful of people and loneliness took a greater hold on my life.

I stopped trying to make friends, therefore I had none. I dreaded attending school and would sometimes wake up and pretend to be ill so I wouldn't have to go. My grades were at their lowest. After so many of these fake illnesses, my dad concluded that many times I was not really ill at all, and in most cases I wasn't. He made me go to school anyway. Out of his anger he would consistently tell me *"you'll never be anything."* In retrospect, I did not see the value in his condescending comments, as expressions of inferiority resonated in my soul, but I understood it was just his way. This type of statement was made so often that I soon began to believe it myself. Many times I found myself looking in the mirror reiterating his very words to myself.

At the age of 16, thoughts of suicide began to emerge in my mind as I thought that no one cared. I began to think of ways to take my life, but I wanted it to be as painless as possible. Then it came to me. My dad was on lots of medication; I would just down a bottle of it and wait for the effects. After some time of taking the drugs, I felt the effects of drunkenness and once that wore off, the self-worthlessness was still there and so was the loneliness. A few months later, my parents found out that I was trying to take my own life and sought some help for me. While recovering from the last attempt of overdosed medication, I laid in a hospital bed being evaluated by a fleet of psychiatrist surrounding me; each conducting their own evaluations. Their recommendation to my parents was that I be confined to a psychiatric institution for treatment of depression and anxiety.

Being a minor, the decision had to go before a judge whom approved the confinement for six months. I felt like I was being punished by those who didn't understand me. Once admitted to the psyche ward, I met several young people who were a lot like me, whom had experienced similar feelings and situations. Ironically, this was the first time in years I felt some happiness. Like the adage goes, *"misery loves company."* Among us defeated ones, there was a bond like family. After a six-month holding period, I was released only to be a part of the ruthless world which I walked back into. Back at school, the kids were saying cruel things about me, calling me crazy, and making it known that I had just been released from the crazy house. Although I grinned as if it were a joke, I was not happy and still did not have a desire to live.

I laughed at myself right along with of those who mocked me, not realizing how *"we"* were destroying *"me"* on the inside. By the time I became a senior in high school, my parents and I discussed making a change in my environment. Subsequently, I moved to another town to live with my older sister. That still did not erase the unstable childhood that began an unending trend of masking the fear of rejection that took root in my life. This unhealthy fear ultimately resulted in a life of loneliness and internal pain.

I now realize that sometimes traumatic experiences in a person's childhood can lead them in directions they should not follow as they enter into adulthood. Life had struck me with a sucker punch for so long that the spirit of fear had moved in with squatters rights. I had succumbed to the onset of inferiority, inadequacy and feared of what others thought of me, as a result of years of ridicule, peer pressures and torment. These haunting experiences caused me to adapt a lifestyle of lies, believing that living through one abusive relationship in exchange for another was better than being alone. The insurmountable loneliness I endured was like a deceiving spirit pushing me to look for love in all the wrong places. Practically any gesture of affection would satisfy me, as long as it stuck around for a while.

When I returned home after high school graduation to start college, my constant tormentors, timidity, rejection and a fear of men had returned to visit. I was reminded of the abuse I endured in the early years from the men in my life. Thinking I had finally escaped my wilderness, I married a man whom I had given myself to, only after becoming pregnant out of wedlock with his child. The romance and love in our marriage was short lived, as I suffered the rugged hand of physical and mental abuse in this relationship. To avoid the embarrassment and shame of what others would say about me, I pleaded with him to stay, at any cost. He remained for a while because of the child that we had conceived. However, he consistently expressed that his desire for me was dead.

The beatings continued, but I did not care. I simply needed to feel as if I belonged to somebody and I did not want others to talk about me. Noticing this marriage was headed for disaster, I thought if I could relocate my family, we could start our lives over again in an unfamiliar environment and things would get better.

We relocated, but not without its challenges and once again my old tormentors' rejection and fear resurfaced. We moved to a larger city and I began to look for work as a musician. The music competition was enormous for a small town girl like me, who only played sheet music. Back home, I was the big fish in the small pond; I was the church choir musician, played for a lot of weddings and was a soloist. I assumed it would be easy to make some quick money in a larger city until I landed a fulltime job. I understood sheet music very well, but that was not enough compared to those that played by sound.

I can recall an interview I had at a local Black church. I was auditioning to play for their youth choir. That interview ended when the youth expected me to play more hip-hop tunes (of which I could not) and insultingly *"booed"* me out. The pastor thanked me for my time and suggested that the arrangement would not work out. Once again rejected, I smiled through my hurt feelings, thanked everyone and left. After leaving, I felt that I had lost the one thing that people really liked about me, my music. From that day forward I never played again.

It is human nature to feel a need to belong. I was no different, only my desire was strong. I needed something or someone else to help me overcome the pain and loneliness experienced in my life. I was not receiving the love and attention I desired at home, so after starting a new job, I began to smoke cigarettes. It became a daily routine. Smoking made me feel as if I belonged. I began to fit in with the other substance abusers on the job. Unfortunately, for me I continued to suffer through the beatings of my husband until we finally went our separate ways. I was left even the more vulnerable.

My vulnerability led me to an adulterous relationship with a man I worked with, who seemed to understand me and desired to be around me. In time, we were married and this marriage was worst than the first one. My desire to belong made me subject to yet another cycle of abuse, only this time, both the children and I were subjected to constant verbal and physical abuse. Nicotine became my companion and I found refuge in retreating to my room smoking cigarette after cigarette. This spouse was even less caring than the first. There were times that he would not come home at night. He wouldn't call either.

Now that you've heard the worst, allow me to tell you the best. You may be asking, *where was God is in all this?* Well, I'll tell you. God was with me all the time, trying to protect me from some things He knew I would encounter as a result of my disobedience. God had to show me that He knew what was best for me, because I had always assumed that I and I alone knew what was best for me. It was that attitude that caused me to retreat to a wilderness of loneliness and pain. While in the wilderness I created, the enemy did not want me to recognize that God was still with me. The enemy had me thinking that, nobody, not even God cared about me. Many of you have experienced wilderness situations in your own lives and questioned God's very existence. I too have sometimes entertained these very same thoughts. At times, I would even get an attitude with God and question His motive for allowing good things to happen for people around me whom I felt did not deserve His blessings. I soon learned through many of my struggles that it was a battle of faith.

While in battle, I engaged in one disastrous experience after another. I felt a strong need to be validated by others, and an overwhelming need to feel a sense of belonging to something that would fill the empty void in my life. The truth of the matter is, I do belong. I belong to God. You see, sometimes we allow people and things to occupy the space in our lives where only God needs to dwell. That was me, bowing to the tactics of deceivers to feel like my cup was full; only to find that it was still empty because I had not invited God to enter in. Some of the things I got myself into, I had no other choice but to pray that God would get me out.

Now that I have found my way back to God, I have repented of all the sins I have committed; those against God and those against myself. In order to be delivered from the torment of my humiliating past I had to:

1. First surrender my life to God. I had to realize that God had a plan for my life that Satan did not want me to fulfill. Once I realized this, I began to recognize the destructive obstacles Satan placed in my path to keep me from achieving all that God had for me.

2. Next, I had to decide not to let loneliness or a fear of rejection dominate my life.

3. Then, I had to rely on an infilling of the Holy Spirit to be my comforter and keep me connected with God.

4. I had to resist the temptation of loneliness, as God warns us about in 1 Peter 5:8; *"Be sober, be vigilant; because your adversary, the devil walks about like a roaring loin, seeking whom he may devour and we must resist him and be steadfast in the faith."*

   - Faith caused me to realize that God loves me and that I too had to learn to love me. No longer could I be my biggest critic. Often times in life, we come to the false conclusion that people don't like us or may be talking about us behind our backs because we are insecure in ourselves. In actuality, it's a personal issue that we ourselves have and only God can handle it for us. Once we find ourselves in *Him,* all insecurities are erased.

   - Satan deals with the mind, but God deals with the heart. The next time your mind tells you that nobody likes you, allow your heart to tell you that Jesus loves you. Because of the love Jesus has for you, you can feel free to love yourself. Remember, Jesus was hated without a cause. Why would we be any different? So, if you are closing people out of your life for fear that they will one day reject you, I encourage you to tear down those walls and be willing to open yourself up to meet friends. If there is something about you that bothers you and it is within your power to change, change it.

- My weight has always been an issue for me. There is nothing medically wrong to hinder my ability to lose weight, so it is within my power to control it. Search within yourself to identify that "thing" that may be causing you to fear rejection and if it is something that is not within your power, I will tell you in my mother's famous word, *"Pray."*

5. When you pray, make sure that you are praying correctly. Your prayer should be for courage and strength to overcome the fear of rejection, not loneliness itself. It is perfectly okay if it helps you to talk to someone who will listen to you as you release the basis of your pain and loneliness. I know that helps for me.

- If you are affiliated with a church and they have a counseling ministry, contact someone there or some of the church leaders who may be willing to listen to you. Don't use them as a dumping ground, but perhaps they will guide you through prayer that can penetrate heaven.

- Now, on the other hand, if for some reason you feel you do not want your church family to become familiar with your situation, there are a lot of anonymous organizations you can contact for help. Just being real here, Christian or not, there are some people that are just plain judgmental and they will expose your confidential business. The key is to find someone who is trustworthy and has an ability to guide you towards receiving God's favor for your life. It is pointless to talk, just to hear yourself talk; rather seek God's love and reassure yourself in *His* promises through all of life's situations.

Even after taking these steps, there were times when I felt like I was on a downward spiral, but I grabbed hold to God's hand and *He* did not let me fall. *He* will come through for you too. God is faithful to rescue us in *His* time and we must realize that ultimately everything will be alright if we faint not. Isaiah 40:31 said *"But those who wait on the Lord will renew their strength; they shall mount up with wings as eagles; they shall run and not be weary, they shall walk and not faint.*

Since I have given my life to God and am walking in His divine order, I no longer feel my life is not worth living. I now "know" that my life is worth living. There are a whole lot of people who have yet to hear my testimony, so that they too can walk in the fullness of life.

God has pulled me out of the pits of gloom and blessed me to live a prosperous life. I was told that I would never amount to anything, but look at me now. God has blessed me with a peaceful home; I've been delivered from smoking cigarettes; I own my own business; I am on the road to success with my educational studies and will earn my first college degree with honors in the summer of 2009. God is good! The blessings in my life continue to flow in my life because I love God and *He* loves me. *He* sustained me even in the times when I tried to destroy my very life.

I'm not out of the woods completely, but I thank God for where I am. I still experience some depression and loneliness, however, the process in which I handle the situation today is totally different from the methods of my past. God is able to keep my mind in perfect peace as long as I keep my mind on Him. My message to others, who may be experiencing a similar wilderness situation, or feel that life is not worth living is to:

- Hold God to His promise to never leave you nor forsake you and remember that you are never truly alone, for God is always with you (Hebrews 13:5).

- Cast your cares upon God for He cares for you like none other (1 Peter 5:7).

- You need to understand that no one or nothing can truly fill that lonely void in your life except for God. Therefore, you must have a relationship with Him.

Having a relationship with God truly makes all the difference.

PRESSING THE MARK

by Toni Emehel

Rejection is often like an unknown tongue spoken by one person that requires translation by another who has been divinely gifted to understand it. Experiencing the rejection of a natural father should redirect one to the heavenly *FATHER* who knows everything about you, yet gave up all that *HE* loved to gain your love.

God wants us to draw near unto *HIM*. Where earthen vessels fail, one must realize that God is the complete expression of love that so many are seeking in their lives. Once you find love in *HIM*, you will not lean heavily on the love and acceptance of others to fuel your soul.

PONDERING THOUGHTS

As an offspring of God, you were fearfully and wonderfully made in *HIS* image and likeness. God wants to show you great and marvelous things in life, but you must first accept *HIM*. Once you have accepted Christ, *HE* will be your biggest encourager, comforter and protector. Won't you accept *HIM* in your life today?

Guilt and Shame

by
Sheria Lofton

GUILT AND SHAME

Be not afraid of their faces: for I am with thee to deliver thee, saith the LORD.

—Jeremiah 1:8

"Momma, momma, don't leave me," I cried. I begged and pleaded for her not to leave. Momma was gone, and it was very, very dark. I couldn't see anything. Nothing was moving, not even the mice or should I say rats. It was so quiet that I could only hear the drips from the faucet and the beating of my little heart.

As I lay there crying myself to sleep, I had hoped momma would come back and rescue me from the dangers that awaited me. She was so caught up in her own little world that my needs were not important to her. She never even stopped to think why her daughter was sobbing.

I heard footsteps coming closer and closer. I lay there pretending to be dead. I would much rather be dead than to encounter what was ahead. As I lay there trying not to breathe, it happened. Like a thief in the night, he robbed me of my innocence. How could momma leave me? She was supposed to protect and keep me safe from harm and danger. Isn't that what real mothers do?

Why God? Why God? Why me? I was only five years old. I didn't understand what had happened to me. I could not articulate the pain that was afflicted upon me. I felt so alone, and I couldn't trust anyone. Whom could I trust when the one I have trusted all my life has left me? I had to question momma's love for me. If momma has left me and I am flesh of her flesh and bones of her bones, I was sure God would leave me too. I had no one I could talk to or share what I had experienced. Did anyone even care?

I started carrying guilt and shame before I had learned to spell my name. I used school as my outlet. This was a place I could feel safe, a hiding place. Wanting to be worthy of being liked and wanting to be better than all the other students, I became an over-achiever in school but withdrawn at home. I was masking my pain through education at an early age.

One day momma said that we were moving from New York to North Carolina. I was so excited. It was the happiest day of my life. This was my great escape from molestation. This was the freest feeling I had ever experienced. Yes, yes, this nine-year-old was free! One would have thought somebody had given me my freedom papers from slavery, but this freedom was teaching me how to run from my problems.

As time went on, momma and I had a love/hate relationship. I wanted her to feel my hurt, pain, guilt and shame. How could I forgive her for leaving me? Maybe she was doing the best she knew how. Maybe it was something that happened to her mother's mother or her mother or even to her. Maybe it was a generational curse. Whatever the case, I knew it had to stop with me.

Years went by and my little body was developing. I was a teenager still carrying guilt and shame only to encounter more pain. I had to figure things out the hard way. I had a hard time understanding God. If He loved me, then why was I encountering so much pain? All those feelings and emotions were bottled up inside me. I wanted to take my life because I did not want to carry the hush, hush secrets of the past anymore. I wanted to share my secret, but I didn't know how to talk about it or explain it. Severe depression and crying became a big part of my life. I was a ticking time bomb ready to explode. Since the issues of the past were never dealt with and I didn't know how to cope, I became rebellious.

As I developed into a young woman, no one ever told me I was of value and that my life had a purpose. I was never told by anyone that I was loved and that I was beautiful. Adding fuel to an already out of control fire, I started looking for love in all the wrong places. I felt I was damaged goods. I hated myself. Somebody should have saved me from that night. *Momma, where were you? God, did you love me?* To this day I am still struggling with trusting people.

When I became a grown woman, I decided to open up and share secrets from my past, my "hush, hush" secret pain. I shared it with momma. She was in disbelief. She wanted to know: *when, where, why* and *who*. That was not quite the response I was expecting. I turned back to that five year old little girl, wanting to hear her say she was sorry for leaving me and putting her own pleasure before my safety. I wanted her to hold and comfort me and tell me everything would be all right. I didn't want her to tell a soul. I just wanted to lie in her arms and cry like a baby.

Momma confronted one of the molesters. He only lied and denied having molested me. I told her I choose to forgive him anyway because I could no longer carry this guilt and shame that was killing me inside. It had robbed me of so much of my childhood, peace, joy, happiness, love, value and relationships.

Another molester did apologize. Just hearing those words made my heart happy. I didn't want to continue going through life seeing him and his continuing to act as if nothing had happened. That would be a slap in the face. Thank God for closure because it brought healing.

I often wonder what my life would be like if I had not encountered these experiences. Did it shape and mold me into the woman I am today? What life lesson was I supposed to learn from this? There are countless women, teenagers and younger girls who have had this same kind of story. I wonder how many are still carrying this kind of burden. How many of them have taken the secret to their grave?

When one is emotionally shipwrecked, any encountered relationship is affected. Hurting people hurt others. It may not be intentional, but one wants to hurt another because he/she is hurt. But no matter what is encountered in this life, life has value and purpose. God created each of us for His purpose and His purpose only. The enemy has tried to destroy many of us at an early age, but we are still standing, still victorious and still vibrant beings.

God has blessed the strained relationship between my momma and me through answered prayers. Momma and I have a wonderful relationship now. We went from enemies to being best friends. The lines of communication are open, and we are able to talk about a lot of things. What Satan meant for evil, God has turned to good.

No matter what cards you have been dealt in life, the choice is yours to overcome or to be defeated.

PRESSING THE MARK

by Toni Emehel

The antics of generational curses are not easily detected. They take away your quality of life and often give you a false sense of being functional until God sends something to prove otherwise. A generational curse is nothing more than a continuous cycle of failure, rooted in the sins of ones ancestral past that have been passed down from one generation to the next. This vicious cycle typically follows the same path of destruction, swaddled in a root sin, with some variation based on the individual and generation affected.

In order to break a generational curse you must:

1. Have the truth to void the lie which has kept your family bound. This can only be done by reading and studying the *Word* of God on specific issues that affect you.
2. Address your personal sins as well as those of your family.
3. Live a life of forgiveness. Forgive yourself and others.
4. Accept God's healing and be released to enjoy life.
5. Live a life of holiness, give no room for sin.

Taking these simple steps is sure to break any existing generational curses that may exist in your life and prevent the deployment of any new-fangled curses for the generations to come.

PONDERING THOUGHTS

Are you living a life of holiness? What steps are you taking to prevent deployment of generational curses in your family that could result as a consequence of a sinful lifestyle?

This is my love story and I dedicate it to the many young military families who are actively involved in providing service to our country.
—Lydia Hilt Clay

Letters from the Sands

by

Lydia Hilt Clay

LETTERS FROM THE SANDS

"For though I am absent in body, yet I am with you in spirit, rejoicing to see your good order and the firmness of your faith in Christ."   *--Colossians 2:5*

"No woman could steal your man like Uncle Sam," was the saying that army wives coined as a result of being separated from their husbands who were deployed on military assignments. I never imagined that one day Uncle Sam would make his move on my man immediately into my marriage, disrupting our relationship.

The year was 1990, and I was abruptly thrust into the journey of my life. We had only been married for a few short months, when my husband began to make preparations for his soon deployment to the Persian Gulf War. It was time to put on the whole armor of God and stand on His promises, like never before.

This is my story about how God sustained me while being separated from my husband. My life during that period was chronicled through a journal of letters from my husband, which I refer to as "Letters from the Sands." These letters privately reflected my inner feelings about the Persian Gulf War and its effects on my relationship with my husband. It is my hope that sharing this wilderness journey will strengthen those families who are still separated from their spouses and loved ones due to serving in military assignments abroad.

My husband, Val, and I were eager to explore our future together as husband and wife. We made many plans that would soon be delayed. After arriving at his first permanent assignment, he had received notice that he would be deployed to the Persian Gulf. On the day that he received his orders, he called to tell me of his news. He started the conversation by prefacing it with, "I have some good news and some bad news." Sometimes surprises caused me to be cautious, so I braced myself and anxiously told him to just tell me. When he told me of the assignment, my mind drew a blank and I really didn't hear much after that moment. I felt my heart stop beating for a moment and drop to the pit of my stomach, as time seemed to stand still. My brain rewound memories faster than a movie trailer. For the moment I was angry and terrified. The tears began to well up in my eyes as I tried to speak, but the words initially would not come forth. My emotions were on full display and even though he could not see my tears, he could hear them over the phone in my voice. I hesitantly shared my fears and uttered the words, "I'm afraid." He affectionately said, *"Baby girl please don't cry, I need you to be strong and look at the bright side, this will soon be over and we can get on with our lives. Remember our plans and dreams, I don't always know how but some how I will show you the world. This is just a momentary interruption and I promise you, my Nubian queen, I'll come back to you. Will you promise to wait for me? Promise me you'll try to stay strong and be the lady I know you are inside."* I began to feel a little more at ease as we prayed together. I also reassured him that, as I had pledged my vows, all my love was devoted to him and together we could weather this storm and when he returned I would be there waiting for him.

After talking with Val, I began to wonder if this was really the life that I had said "*I do*" to. The uncertainties of being a military wife were beginning to unfold. I always considered myself to be a fighter and I was determined to hold on to my dreams with unwavering faith in God.

While Val was away training for his deployment to the Persian Gulf, I became intensely focused on my studies. I aggressively sought to bring completion to the college program I was involved in. Val wrote me letters, informing me of the preparations he was making for me to settle into a new home during his absence. It made me feel proud to know that he was a husband who did not want me to be worried about anything during his absence. I missed him more than anyone could know.

To ease the burden and pain of being without Val, I made plans, to visit him during the semester break and prior to his deployment. This trip would afford me the opportunity to become familiar with the military base, which I would soon call home. While I was with Val, I prayed that time would hold still, just to have a few more moments with him. It felt so comforting to lay in the cradle of his warm arms, feeling his love embrace me softly. We made time to invest in our love and create loving memories. We spent a day at the beach and took time to go over all the necessities that I would have to manage in his absence.

Although our visit was brief, it was a treasure to hold. As I packed to return to college, my mind raced back and forth over the uncertainties to come. Yet I knew that I would have to be strong. Fighting back the tears, I was not ready for him to leave. The challenge was calming my inner fears and anxieties about our separation. Neither of us wanted to say the first goodbye, so we hugged each other tightly and said a hopeful "I'll see you later".

It would be several weeks between our visit and the actual deployment, but the date seemed to arrive so quickly. Val phoned to say his goodbyes and again encourage me to stay strong and remain prayerful. He told me about all the soldiers in his platoon and how he was the comic relief to keep the troops focused on their mission. When the unit had to board the plane, he whispered, *"you know I love you and I am sending you a 1000 kisses, special delivery by God."* He asked me to give him one of those million dollar smiles that he loved and he would feel it in his heart and know that I was alright. I told him I loved him, I would pray for him and that he must stay alert, stay alive and come back to me. Later that night, I fervently prayed and asked God to please protect him always, bring him back safe and unharmed. Because I was alone and missed him so, I knew that this journey would be a test of sheer faith and commitment for me. I gently tucked my pillow and fell asleep with tears silently rolling down my cheeks.

Later, I reassured myself that God would definitely sustain us as He had done many times before. Like the story of Esther in the bible,

I knew that I could not lie around mopping about the situation, but my new life would bring many tests of faith and consultations with God. The Holy Spirit had revealed to me that as we began this journey in our relationship, it would be essential for us to put on the full armor of God. It would not be by my own strength that I would prevail, but through the grace of God and the guidance of the Holy Spirit. And then I would be able to accomplish all things through Christ. During this difficult season it became evident that we needed to apply five important elements to sustain one another, which were: *Communication, Trust, Faith, Prayer and Creating Memories* which would map out the course for us to survive the challenges of this long distant relationship.

Reflecting on the memories of our honeymoon, I remembered a conversation about open communication which is a mainstay of any lasting relationship. So, I immediately began to write letters to let him know that he was on my mind. Curled up in one of his old pair of pajamas, still scented with his fragrance, I began to sense that his presence was somehow very near. It inspired me to write one of my initial letters which expressed the love of two hearts beating as one. When I placed the stamp on the letter, I sealed it with at kiss and sprayed a touch of my perfume over it. My intent was to ignite within him pleasurable thoughts and sensual memories.

I also wrote intimate handwritten notes to Val and letters that informed him about daily affairs to keep him in touch with things at home. Someone once said that handwritten letters always added a personal touch and a sentiment that spoke from the heart. This was the reason I intentionally sent handwritten letters to Val, because I wanted to lavish him with the deep love of my heart.

Many of the letters that Val sent me were from the war zone.

There was sometimes a film of desert dust on them. He often wrote about the bad desert storms they were experiencing, where everything would be covered with desert sand. In this particular letter he called me his "distant lover" and wrote:

"I love you so, when I think of you I start to explode. How will you know that I love you -- through my words, my actions and my feelings? I treasure our relationship. It's like gold. I can't wait to come back. WOW! There are so many things that I want to say when I think of our reunion. Oh, my baby, I just can't help writing words like that. For now it's the best way I can explain this feeling. I think of the times we walked together in the sand on the beach. A lot of people think badly of the sand, I walk alone thinking "have you seen her?" It's like I'm lost here without you. As I walk looking at the stars sayings, "she left her kiss upon my lips, I can feel her arms reaching towards me, but I can't see her." As the day comes to an end I think "I'll find her in my dreams".

It was letters like this that made me remember the foundation on which our relationship was established. Val was a funny guy, a free spirit, unafraid to experience life. And reading his letters I knew that there was no doubt that he truly loved me.

Our letters were a way to expose our hearts without regret. Some were more endearing than others, but yet we could see the beauty and love God intended a marriage to have. We thought so much of one another and prayed daily for the welfare of each other, even to the point of dreaming of each other on occasion. We began to create fond memories that would give us strength during tough times and help us to sustain our relationship in the years to come. I mused that, one day in the future, we would look back and laugh and say our love was as strong as the sea and we had the faith to know that God was at the center of it all ensuring that it would never die.

Once Val wrote to me the following:

"Dear Sweetheart, you lovely thing: Guess what? You may not understand this but you kissed me on my back this morning. Right before I woke up, I was asleep in my sleeping bag with my undershirt off. I had never done that, since it has been cold here, but I did so last night. Well while I was sleep I felt just a simple soft kiss on my back. It was as real as this paper I write on. When I felt that kiss, I immediately woke up and I was still in the sleeping bag. You know the Lord works in mysterious ways and this morning I got a kiss from you while still asleep. I started praying a prayer of Thanksgiving because I knew that it was truly miraculous. Your lips felt so sweet, like only the Lord and I knew it could be. I was thinking I shouldn't say anything, to anyone because no one would ever believe it."

While reading Val's letter, desire seemed to overwhelm me. I felt as if I were lying next to his strong muscular body, curled up together as we had often done. I imagined that Val had the stamina of Samson. Without fail he knew just how to heat up my nights with his intense passion. So, in the poetry of his passionate letters I understood the desires he was expressing. I knew that Val trusted me with his innermost thoughts and allowed me to be the caretaker of his passion. I felt that he trusted me to remain faithful to the vows we exchanged on our wedding day. Trust was essential for our marriage as with any marriage, for without it the foundation would be weak.

I wrote to Val about my many distractions in college and how my faith seemed to be subsiding. For some reason I felt the need to share with him some of the frustrations I was going through. Then the fear of loss came upon me and I remembered my mother's words encouraging us to pray and trust God to do what was best for my family. So I prayed and encouraged myself in the scriptures:

This I call to mind and therefore I have hope; because of the Lord's great love we are not consumed, for his compassions never fail. They are new every morning; great is your faithfulness. (Lamentations 3:21-23) and *Cast your cares on the Lord and he will sustain you; he will never let the righteous fall.* (Psalm 55:22)

During this time of separation it was important for me to fortify my faith with actions and prayer. My consistent prayer life was talking to God, who was my rock and this was what nurtured my soul.

There I was living in Savannah, Georgia in the home Val had prepared for me. Standing in the midst of my combined office and guest bedroom, I was consumed with my thoughts. I remembered reading the power of attorney document that he had left behind, when reality knocked at my door. In the battling of my mind I struggled with the reality of what all this really meant. I was now in control of all my husband's personal assets. I felt my heart beating outside of my chest with mixed emotions and all at once fear seized me. My mind was captivated with doubtful thoughts of the "what if's". I began to question my own abilities. I asked myself, what if something happened to Val. What if he came home with a disability? What if he didn't come back at all, then what? My inner spirit was determined to conquer the doubt of the "what if's" that were haunting me. I knew I had to get a grip and have faith in God. I stopped to pray and asked God: *"Please dear God, hear my cry, I don't know why I am feeling this way, but please keep my husband safe, and let no hurt, harm or danger come near him. Allow your angels to encamp around and about him wherever he should go. Protect him from the enemy, supply his every need and provide us both with wisdom in decision making".* After spending time in prayer, I fell asleep in peace and believed that God had truly heard my prayer.

Val's letters also served to strengthen and encourage me. I was able to grasp the reigns to take control of my destiny and our future. Having a renewed sense of purpose and more courage, I was motivated to get involved in the military community where I lived. I visited the local community center as a first step. I had a desire to help others and wanted to focus on being a problem solver. There was a community information board in the center and a help-wanted ad for a volunteer

Financial Planner. I also felt that this would be a good way to reinforce my own personal commitment to building wealth. Applying the knowledge gain in college, I began to teach other military family members about personal financial management. I found this activity to be fulfilling as it allowed me to support others. I was reminded of how the apostle Paul encouraged the people to persevere in the works of Christ and be diligent in well-doing; and how to find peace and contentment in a perilous world. I enjoyed the volunteer work and the feeling of usefulness it provided me.

I then decided to participate in the military wives social circle. I continued to find solace in writing almost daily to Val, sharing the events of my day, replying to his letters and reassuring him that everything was going well with me. In associating with other military wives, I learned that discernment in written communication was very important in a long distance relationship. A wise woman shared that the soldiers face an enormous amount of stress and daily pressures from the hostile environments in which they work. Therefore, as wives and loved ones, we did not want to further complicate or endanger their well-being by sending unnecessary stressful communications. Our husbands needed our support to help maintain a balance for them to remain focused on their priorities abroad.

Searching for ways to fill the void in my life had become a challenge for me. I no longer found fulfillment in my association with the other military wives. Many of them had infants and small children as their primary focus; as a result many activities were centered on children events. I didn't have children; therefore, I felt a bit awkward trying to fit in. Despite the fact that I had come from a large family and always had a love for children. Val wrote me a letter sharing his vision of having a family:

"If you want children I am ready. If you want to, I think that it is even better to wait until after you have settled into your first job. I can live with whatever makes you happy. I just feel that after this I would like to start a family. A little baby, the two of us can enjoy, roll around on the floor and play with, of course we would have to take turns changing diaper (smile). We would teach the baby good manners and go for walks together with the baby in the stroller. You know I really enjoy thinking about things like that. It makes me feel special, and we both will have something to look forward to – anyway I just wanted to tell you that I love you very much."

Deeply pondering several thoughts, I questioned our reasons for wanting to wait, could I have been wrong to want to wait? What consequences would be the result of waiting? Will I have the opportunity that so many married couples say is the ultimate beautiful bonding experience in a marriage? Deep within I felt that I had so much love to give and so many gifts to share with a child. I also had heartbreaking doubtful thoughts of "What if?" What if Val doesn't come back to make our having a child a possibility? Had I been too selfish with my wanting to wait -- wait until I had established some type of career? I thought it was too soon after marrying, I needed time to enjoy my husband and we needed time to learn each other and get better acquainted in this relationship. Then I questioned, was I simply fearful of becoming a mother? Plenty of our friends and relatives seemed to assume that I needed the practice when they left their children in my care. I don't think that they understood that it was my decision not to have a child at that time. Once again I had to minster to myself and recalled scriptures such as, *Jeremiah 29:11 and Psalm 37:3-5*. Then I encouraged myself through the word of the Lord by recalling Hannah's prayers which indicated that Val and I should pray together, be at peace and follow God's plan.

To help fill my day, I began exercising, walking and running with my next door neighbor. She also gave me the tour of the post while we ran and walked our five-mile course. This exercise program became my routine three times a week. Exercise had always been a stress reliever for me as well as keeps me in shape. My relationship with this neighbor grew to be a close friendship that gave me a sense of belonging and eased the pains of loneliness.

After several months, I received a visit from a female soldier from Val's unit, who was on emergency leave. She had promised him that she would visit me and she reassured me that he was doing well. She invited me to attend church with her and assured me that I would love it since we were of the same faith. The people at the church created a real family-like atmosphere and supportive environment. I was introduced to the other families at the service. Through conversation, I found out that Val had met a few of the families prior to my arrival on post and spoke of me often. Some of them indicated that they felt as if they knew me and welcomed me as one of the family.

The church family often sent packages to the soldiers during the holidays. I was glad to have become involved with this church. The veterans in the community also took a stand to make sure that the troops were not forgotten. It was the prayers, support and involvements that helped me cope with the many challenges the war had added to my life. I knew it was a turning point in my life. I had a renewed faith and confidence in my abilities. I gained strength and golden friendships that would last for many years to come. I understood even more the supernatural power of prayer and faith.

Time has a way of maturing our will. Val's written messages of love resonated with me a period of innocence. I wondered could he be auditioning to become a romantic love poet. He wrote on one occasion:

When I look up at the sky and see the beautiful stars, I sometimes wonder if you are on the other side of the world looking at those same beautiful stars. Next time you get a chance look up in the sky at night and say something to me. Believe me I know the Lord will make sure I hear it. I love you so much, I just don't know what to do. I should have married you the first day I met you, that way I could have enjoyed this feeling a few months longer. When I think about our life together I can't help but smile. There is nothing in this world that can change the way I feel about you. My heart is filled to the brim with your love.

My dear husband, Val, had written many letters to me as he had promised to do. Some were so intimately intense that they mentally swept me off my feet. They captured the expressions of his heart and his true feeling about me and our marriage. His love inspired my hope for our future together. I was consumed and carried away with the spirit of our love.

After the unit had completed their tour of duty, my prayers had manifested. I was both excited and anxious with anticipation. I received information about the homecoming of Val and the other soldiers. All day I prepared myself as if it were my wedding day, making sure my appearance was picture perfect for Val.

I waited late into the evening along with other waiting families for our loved ones arrival. I admit, I became impatient as I waited. Val and other officers were some of the last to exit the debriefing areas. Val was dressed from head to toe in full battle gear and desert uniform, and for this reason I did not immediately recognize him, plus it was dark outside. He walked up to me and said, "Hey sexy lady, who do you belong to?" Hearing his voice, I screamed with excitement as I hastily leaped into his arms. He scooped me up off my feet, swirled me around and kissed me passionately. My hero had returned home. To God be the glory!

This is my love story and I dedicate it to the many young military families who are actively involved in providing service to our country. It is my prayer that when you feel challenged in your relationship and your faith is being tested, don't give up! Know that God cares and will not give you more than you can handle. Be encouraged, stay prayerful and strong in your faith and according to your faith, you shall receive. Ask God to open your heart to receive His word and allow the Holy Spirit to be your guide through difficult times.

This wilderness experience may have isolated me with reflections of my thoughts; but it also stimulated growth and maturity within me. I gained renewed strength and gratitude for the solidarity in my relationship with my husband.

5-ACTION STEPS THE HOLY SPIRIT REVEALED TO ME ABOUT LONG DISTANT RELATIONSHIPS

1. **Communication**. Frequent Communication is essential in developing the relationship and opening the way for spiritual intimacy and strengthening the bond of the covenant agreement that you share with your spouse. Write or call when appropriate, share with your lover those things that will encourage and help them to feel secure in the relationship.

2. **Trust**: It is important to provide security within the relationship, be faithful and assure one another that your love is built without an exit clause.

3. **Faith**: Faith is your vision of the future, it is what you hope to see manifested. It is the belief and confidence of knowing, that which you have asked of God shall come to past. Exercise your faith by speaking God's word. Faith comes by hearing, so speak God's promises as well you should write and encourage one another in the scriptures.

4. **Prayer**: The word of God states that we are to always pray. Seek Him daily and consult him about every concern of the heart. Pray consistently for your spouse, their covering, protection and wisdom in decisions making. Get involved with a local church that teaches truth and God's word. This will help you with your spiritual development.

5. **Creative Memories:** Take time to appreciate the gift that God has given you in this relationship. Pause and take time to create mini celebrations, send tokens of love to remind them that you care. Use descriptive words to allow your lover to visualize a special intimate moment. Get involved with local military family support groups and assist with the activities that support our troops.

God is the source of all your needs; make him the center of your relationship and you will see good success.

PRESSING THE MARK

by Toni Emehel

There are five essential factors that make for happiness in marital relationships:

1. Allow God to use you as an instrument to bless your spouse.

2. Love each other unconditionally with forbearance and acceptance.

3. Bare your souls to each other by praying together. This will enhance your level of trust and intimacy toward one another. If you share a distant relationship with your spouse, agree to meet one another in prayer during a set time during the day. It will allow you to uplift each other at the same time in unity and agreement.

4. Remain faithful to the Body of Christ. Find a mutual place of worship, were each of you can grow spiritually. If you share a distant relationship with your spouse make use of resources available to ensure that both of you are being fed from the same spiritual table.

5. Consult one another when making major decisions. Particularly, those that involve finances.

PONDERING THOUGHTS

The blessings and benefits of building a Christian marriage are priceless. Though the five principles above are not exhaustive, they are a good starting point to get your marriage on good footing. If you are not currently practicing these principles in your marriage, come together with your spouse and identify any obstacles barricading your way. Discuss what you can do to begin building a Christian marriage today.

People without a heart for God do not have access to the protection afforded to those who wholeheartedly tread the Highway of Holiness.

—Sadie E. Anderson

Highway through the Wilderness

by

Sadie E. Anderson

HIGHWAY THROUGH THE WILDERNESS

And an highway shall be there, and a way, and it shall be called the way of holiness; the unclean shall not pass over it; but it shall be for those: the wayfaring men, though fools, shall not err therein.

—Isaiah 35:8

I can still remember the open flesh and marred skin etched in my Daddy's back, all in the name of providing for his family. There was nothing that Daddy would not do for us, including putting his life on the line. I stood there behind him in shock, as Mother was caring for his wounds. I was gazing through a child's eyes trying to figure out why Daddy had been beaten so severely. Had he not left that morning to sale the harvest of our tobacco field as he had done many times before? What was different about this time? Well, I'll tell you what was different about this time. My parents, being the strong believers that they were, were under enemy attack to see if they would stray from the straight and narrow.

Above all else, my parents believed in the power of prayer and trained us to believe that no matter the circumstance, prayer to God would always get us through. I can still remember Sunday mornings in the Bridgers home that began with family assembly and prayer just before breakfast. This was no cracker box prayer-time, but a time when we met God with thankful hearts, on bended knee as we prayed for *His* continued blessings and protection over our family.

It was those same prayers that saved Daddy's life on that day when a number of crooks and robbers followed him as he went to the city to sale the tobacco he had harvested. Somewhere between town and his journey home, those crooks ambushed Daddy, took his money and left him for dead. Though Daddy was a man who stood tall, he was a man of short stature. Seemingly, he was easy prey for the robbers. They trampled his flesh and then discarded him like a filthy rag. After they had had their way with him, they covered his butchered body with bushes and tree branches. Then they left my Daddy there to die. I can only imagine the thoughts that ran through Daddy's mind as he laid there stinging with pain as his life drained through open wounds. Of all the things he could have possibly thought and all the words he could have possibly prayed, I'm sure my Daddy's prayers hinged on these words, *"The Lord is my shepherd, I shall not want, I will fear no evil, though I walk through the valley of the shadow of death, I will fear no evil, for thou art with me."* (Psalm 23)

With God at his side, Daddy laid there stiff as a board to encourage his attackers that he was near dead, if not already dead. Can you imagine the insurmountable degree of control one would have to have to muffle sighs of pain from a near death beating? Yet, Daddy laid there still, quiet and profusely bleeding, hanging on to promises of the one whom he call, God.

After splitting up my Daddy's money, the men left. It was at that time that God gave Daddy the strength to lift his body and find his way home. I still can't believe that one human can beat and malign another human's body so badly. I remember looking at my father's back, as his flesh reeked of pain and I hurt for him. Satan tried to kill Daddy on that day, but all he could do was wound him. You see, my Daddy was on a highway where nothing or ANYONE could deter him. As long as he kept his faith and continued to abide in God's word, he may have suffered wounds, but he would always prevail until the Lord determined differently.

My father's wilderness experience was the first of many that showed me how to rightfully position myself for God's protection during the wilderness hikes of my own life. He and my mother did all they knew how to do to make sure each of their 11 children reverenced the Lord. Thinking back, my parents weren't all that, but in a child's eyes a parent can do no wrong. However, one thing they did right was to guide me to Christ so that I would be equipped to face the personal challenges in my life when I got older.

In March 1947, Daddy took ill and God saw fit to call him home. Daddy had a short lived life. He died at the age of 43. I guess he had accomplished all that God had for him on this earth. He was a good God-fearing man who set a godly example of headship in our home. He knew his place and took his manly responsibilities seriously.

When he died, Mother was left alone to nurture and provide for eleven children, all birthed with my father. I was only eleven years old at the time, and little did I know God was providing me with yet another godly example of survival that I would later have to draw from to emerge from the wilds in store for me later on down the road.

No doubt about it, Mother had some pretty big shoes to fill being that she was a housewife and Daddy did everything to provide for our family. Growing up in our home was like being in the Garden of Eden with Adam and Eve. Our parents always provided us with the things we needed and some of the things we wanted. Just as the Bible states: *"He has never seen the seed of the righteous forsaken, or his seed begging for bread,"* well even with eleven children, none of us have ever felt like God had forsaken us and never a day begged for anything. Thinking back, I can not remember a time of wanting anything that was not right at our fingertips. Daddy and Mother saw to that. They were good providers. Daddy knew his place in the house well.

Daddy was the head of the house just as all mankind should be. He harvested all our food on the farm we owned and Mother managed the home. She took care of the children and made most, if not all of our clothes. She was a very skillful seamstress *(a skill I picked up from watching her).* Mother could cut patterns from newspapers and make the most beautiful dresses for my sisters and me. Although we did have to purchase shoes and hosiery items, along with some other things that Mother just didn't want to make *(like clothes for my brothers)*, we rarely had to go to town to buy any clothing.

In fact, because my parents operated in the many talents God had given them, there was very little that our family needed to go to town for. We had become self-sufficient on our 103 acre farm, with an occasional need for milk, flour and other dry products like rice. Daddy raised cows, hogs, goats, chickens and geese. From these things, we were able to produce milk, butter and fresh vegetables and even made money from the sale of some of our agricultural products. So, as you can see there was no need to buy anything from the merchants in town. Growing up for me was just like being in paradise.

This all changed the day Daddy died. Mother didn't have a clue about being independent. She had always been a manager of her household and had no experience with the outside world. Mother was dependent on Daddy to do everything outside of our home. Consequently, she sold the farm Daddy worked so hard to maintain for his family. We had to sell it, because there was no one to work it. Who would have known that some years later, I would tread a similar path of wilderness as my Mother.

I had long dreamed of getting married and having children. My ideal family was one with a husband and four children; two boys and two girls. In my book, this was a complete family. But God's book said differently. This "dream" family was not the family plan *He* designed for me.

I met my husband, Willie, when I was fifteen years of age and we were married before my sixteenth birth date. Back in those days, it wasn't uncommon for girls to marry at such a young age. It was expected. My husband was fifteen years older than me, but he was a good and respectful man. We courted for some time, before he asked Mother for my hand in marriage. She gave us her blessings and told him that if he ever got to the point where he felt like he had to put his hands on me, he could bring me back through the same door that he was taking me out of.

After taking a series of blood tests, we went to the Justice of the Peace office and got married. Life was good and we immediately began working on starting our family. In time, I gave birth to a beautiful baby girl. It seemed like one moment I was nursing her, and the next moment doctors were telling me to prepare for her death. She was only three months old when she died of pneumonia. I was devastated. It seemed that just as I was getting comfortable with the notion of being a mother, my child was literally snatched from my breast.

My parents had taught me the power of prayer, so I knew that God was with me. If *He* saw fit to take this child from me, then surely He would see fit to give me another to take her place. And that is just what he did. In months, I was pregnant again with my second child, this time a son. Shortly after his birth, Willie and I had to uproot the family and move to his father's farm in South Carolina. Willie's father had taken ill and so did my child. The climate change was too much for my baby's young body. Shortly after Willie's father died, so did my child.

I can remember asking God why *He* had forsaken me and taken my second child. I felt like I was being punished for something. Had I not been faithful to *Him?* This child too, was taken from me like the last, died of pneumonia around three months of age. Just when I was starting to build a bond with my children, God took them away from me. Willie reminded me that, *"the Lord giveth and the Lord taketh away."* He reminded me of the story of Job, who had lost all that he had and was required to start all over again. Just like Job, Willie and I were all that we had left standing. But, God is faithful and *He* blessed us to start all over again. Because we were faithful, God blessed us with much more than we lost: 10 beautiful and healthy children; six girls and four boys. Together, my husband and I stood on the promises of God and we were blessed because of it.

Just as I thought God had freed me to escape from one wilderness, little did I know I was trekking upon another. I am so godly proud to say that my parents taught me at an early age that, *"the fear of God is the beginning of wisdom."* I learned, *"to trust in the Lord with all my heart and to lean not unto my own understanding, rather acknowledge Him in all things"* as I allowed *Him* to direct my path through wilderness experiences.

Life has taught me that the wilderness is a dark, cold place where all sorts of wild and scary beast roam. In every wilderness, there is a highway to safety. I rely on Isaiah 35:8 when I say that, *"there is a way, a highway and nothing unclean can get on it".* The King of Kings and the Lord of Lord is on this highway and *He* and only *He* can and will lead us through the wilderness situations affecting our lives. However, in order to obtain God's unmerited protection on the Highway of Holiness, we must learn the way of holiness, which begins with devoting our hearts to *Him.*

People without a heart for God do not have access to the protection afforded to those who wholeheartedly tread the Highway of Holiness. My parents led me to this highway at an early age and I have been treading on it every since. I have never had a fear of sudden danger and have lived a fearless life knowing God's protection and provision was always with me. Sure, I cried out in my wilderness, we all do, but I never strayed from the highway.

Just before I was thrust into the ultimate wilderness experience of my life, I had a vision that I was out in the wild and the Lord was telling me that my journey was not over. I could see my husband, Willie out in the wild too. Then the phone rang and it was Willie's boss, from his job. He was calling to tell me that Willie had been in an accident. Willie had gotten his left arm caught in a wood cutting machine at the saw mill he worked at. Willie's arm had been fed into the machine all the way up to his elbow.

After being examined at the hospital, doctors told us that Willie didn't have any broken bones, but they wanted to keep him for observation. That was a Thursday, by Friday, Willie's hand was so severely swollen that it looked as if his fingers were going to burst. By Sunday, Willie's injury had gotten worse but the doctors were holding firm that it was just a bad cut and that there were no broken bones. I was very young at the time and didn't have any experience in tending to matters of this kind. I didn't know what to do, all I knew was that my husband's arm was getting worse and it did not appear that the doctors were doing anything about it!

Willie was in and out of consciousness, but the Lord gave him just enough strength to instruct me to call his boss on the job to tell him to take Willie away from that place! After Willie threatened to discharge himself, his boss showed up and took Willie to Duke Hospital in Durham, North Carolina. While at Duke, doctors examined and treated Willie for gangrene and amputated his arm, all the way up to his shoulder, before I could arrive. It was downhill for Willie from that day on.

It was three months before Willie returned home to our family. He came home without the security blanket *(the comfort of the arm he used to cradle me)* I used to find so much comfort in as he cradled me while I was asleep. Willie was going through a wilderness of his own. God was trying to draw him in, but Willie wasn't coming without a fight. Willie wasn't a bad man he just had some bad habits that were keeping him separated from God. As a result, Willie's wilderness became my wilderness.

While we were both struggling for survival, I found my way to holiness. I met a lady who invited me to prayer meeting. I went, because I knew I needed something else in my life. I had been baptized at the age of 12, but something was missing. It was at these prayer meetings that I gave my heart to God. I wanted so much to share the peace I found in the Lord with Willie, but he would not go to church with me. So, every time I would go to church, I would go to the altar and pray for my husband to give his life to the Lord.

Willie sat by quietly and watched me take the children to church, night after night, Sunday after Sunday until one day he was humbly persuaded to lay down his sinful ways and dedicate his life to the Lord. One night, after he came in from work, Willie put on his clothes for church. For the first time ever, we attended church as a family. While there, Willie confessed his sins to God and asked for forgiveness. On that night, Willie turned his life over to *Him.*

Not long after that, Willie began serving God with a passion I've never seen before. He was played his guitar during worship services, he was head of the Deacon Board and God blessed him to be able to go back to work so that he could provide for our family. Willie was able to do all of this with a make-shift arm that filled the space of the arm he had lost.

Then the devil launched an attack against Willie physically. It was one attack after another, eventually Willie was unable to work at all. It was at that time that the traditional roles in our family shifted. I had to transition from being a housewife to a working wife and primary breadwinner. I, like my mother, had always been a manager of my home. I did not associate with many people outside of church folk and family, but I had to do something so my family could survive *(sound familiar…my mother's footsteps)*.

Willie had suffered two strokes that left him paralyzed. He was unable to walk or talk for some time. If our family was going to survive, I had to go outside the home to find work. With the Lord guiding my footsteps, I did not have to look far. The first company I went to, Carolina Overhalls Company, hired me on the spot. Though the company later changed its name, I worked there until the day I retired using the skills I learned from my mother, as a seamstress.

Willie never regained his health and I took care of him along with our ten children all by myself. We never received any assistance from the government and I can truly say that God supplied our every need. We never missed a meal, had clothes on our back and always had a warm place to lay our heads. All of my children graduated from high school and went on to lead successful lives. That's not to say that some of them didn't go astray, because they did. And when they strayed, God was there with them on my behalf.

As for Willie, he remained faithful to the Lord in his final days. His prayer to God during this time was not for healing, but for a life extension. Willie wanted to live long enough to see his baby girl able to take care of herself. At that time, the baby was only a year old. The Lord spoke to Willie and told him that *He* would add fifteen more years on to Willie's life. Prior to the time Willie passed, not only was our baby girl able to take care of herself, but she would rush home from school each day to take care of him too. Exactly fifteen years after the Lord promised to extend Willie's life, our baby daughter turned sixteen and God took Willie home. You can't tell me God ain't real! If He ain't real, someone else needs to be writing this story!

God gave my husband just what *He* spoke to him. *He* also answered my prayers by providing and protecting my family during a time when we had no headship other than me. I am a devout believer that the only reason my family didn't suffer tremendous attacks of the enemy while in the wilderness periods of our lives is because Willie and I rightfully placed our family onto the *Highway of Holiness* for God's protection and provision. You too can establish a hedge of protection for you and your family, if you: dedicate your heart to Christ, dedicate your every work to *His* glory and align your pathways with *His* word *(this means allowing the word of God to be a lamp unto your feet)*. Don't take my word for it, open your Bible and read it yourself. Below, I have included a list of scriptures that I would like you to set aside 15 minutes each day to read and digest so that you too can walk in the fullness of protection of our Lord and Savior.

SCRIPTUAL STUDY
- Isaiah 35:8-18
- Ephesians 6:10-18
- Titus 2
- Proverbs 31:10-12; 26-30
- Psalms 37:23-27
- Psalms 1:28-3
- Job 1:8-21

As you read these scriptures, think on how you can apply the biblical principles involved to navigate the wilds of your own life.

PRESSING THE MARK

by Toni Emehel

Man was created to glorify God. God desires to be distinctly recognizable in all that we do and all that we choose not to do. One of the greatest rewards of living a life that glorifies God is that we can live the abundant life in the midst of life's wilderness situations. Listed below are some practical ways to live a life that glorifies God:

1. Confess your sins to God and enter into a covenant relationship with *Him* (Romans 10:9).
2. Commit every aspect of your life to Him (Colossians 1:10).
3. Communicate God's word to others (2 Thessalonians 3:1).

PONDERING THOUGHTS

Is God's presence in your life clearly recognizable? Have you committed every aspect of your life to Him? Take an introspective look at your life and pray for godly wisdom in allowing God to direct the flow of your life towards Him (Proverbs 3:24; Thessalonians 4:1-2).

Fleeing from Woman

by

Toni Emehel

FLEEING FROM WOMAN

"I call heaven and earth to record this day against you, that I have set before you life and death, blessing and cursing: therefore choose life, that both thou and thy seed may live."

—*Deuteronomy 30:19*

A cold surgical Babcock and mincing scalpel were the instruments of choice I used to sharply and bluntly excise God's blessings from my life. It was on that day that my most significant features were carted away in a simple clear plastic container; one marked in yellow ink to show that the attending physician did just as I directed him to do, *"destroy them both so that I may no longer reproduce."* It was my flawed human nature that caused me to close myself off from God's blessings. Even with a sound moral base built on a Christian upbringing, I did not realize that the willful act of maiming my reproductive system to achieve permanent sterilization, *(having my fallopian tubes tied and cut)* was a moral sin against God. A sin rooted in rebellion, disobedience and an outright refusal to take on the image of Christ.

My elective lifestyle of barrenness told God that I placed a greater value on pleasing my flesh than I had placed on being the life-giving vessel *He* had designed me to be. At the time I committed this dishonoring act of sin, I was just two days into my twenty-second year of life. I had been married for three and a half years, roughing it through life and did not have a clue as to my God-given purpose. God had designed my body in perfect working order, with each system carrying out its intended function without disruption or fail. *He* had already blessed me with two wonderful gifts, both daughters, one of which I had just given birth to a few hours prior to consummating one of the most critical decisions of my life.

As I marveled at the perfect mold of sweetness bundled in my arms, my heart overflowed with the joy of being a new mother. Like most, I proudly declared my precious newly born child, as yet another gift from God. With nearly every congratulatory call or visit I received, there was the following resounding question and answer,

"Girl, are you going to get your tubes tied? I know I would." (Now-a-days this is one of the most commonly asked delivery room questions by medical providers tending any woman who has given birth to two or more children; married or not.)

While most applauded my decision to immediately bar my womb, there was a lone voice that cautioned me to reconsider. Though her words to me lacked any biblical reference she cared enough to warn me that I may live to regret my decision. She knew first hand of my strained marital relationship. She lovingly cautioned me to consider keeping my reproductive system in tact for the possibility that I may one day have a change of heart and/or desire to have children with a different husband in a future marriage.

The paradox of it all is that while I was fleeing from being the woman God created me to be, I received more encouragement from non-believers who applauded and encouraged me to follow through with this life-disparaging decision while I did not receive any encouragement or guidance from believers who should have been directing me to follow God's plan for my life. There were no ministers, missionaries, evangelist, pastors or outreach workers at my bedside who did not mind *"getting in my business"* and challenging my professed beliefs that children are gifts from God. Though I did not realize it then, I now realize that if we as Christians truly believe that children are gifts from God there would be no way any of us could follow through with surgical procedures to achieve reproductive sterilization.

God and God alone *"is"* and *"should be"* the author and giver of life. *He* created husband and wife (man and woman) to be fruitful and multiply. Who are we to tell God that *He* does not know what *He* is doing by attempting to keep *Him* from doing what *He* desires to do through us? That is exactly what we do when we take measures to seal our reproductive capacity.

It is my sincere prayer that by sharing this personal narrative on how God changed my heart regarding a common practice embraced by many Christian men and women, people all over the world will be provoked to think biblically about the offense and act of sin involved with medically altering one's reproductive system to prevent childbirth. The pages that follow contain a delicate look at how this single act of sin separated me from God and set me on a journey that led to the discovery of God's faithfulness and forgiveness (1John1:19). It is my desire that the sharing of this chapter of my life will encourage men and women to seek the mind of Christ in all things including the use of voluntary sterilization measures.

****

Nine years had passed. I was divorced and entering my second marriage with the man of my dreams, a true Godsend. He was purpose driven, confident in his identity and most importantly, he had a personal relationship with Christ. Early in our dating relationship my husband made it clear that he wanted to father children. The fact that I had sealed my womb from bearing children did not curtail his desire to marry and produce children with me in the future.

After a six year dating relationship, a wedding date was set. Though our marriage did not have a written prenuptial agreement, we did have a meeting of the minds to contend with my infertility. We did not have a set time or date to deal with it, but we agreed that early in our marriage we would explore options to have my fertility restored. After a year-long search we found a team of medical physicians who were considered the best in their field. In June 2000, some 10 years after an attempt to bar my womb, and just one year after our marriage, I found myself sprawled out in regret. I was lying on a cold surgical steel table, drifting off into bright reflector lights that illuminated my body, petitioning God to restore the fertility I had so carelessly discarded.

The act of rectifying my past wrong seemed honorable, but sadly, it was not biblical. The sole reason I was going through this procedure was to please and fulfill the desires of my husband. After a "successful" surgery we returned home with my fertility restored and with high hopes of conceiving our first, second and third child together. Unfortunately, as you read further, you will find that because my decision had no biblical basis it resulted in me drawing my husband deep into the wilderness right along side of me.

In the spring of 2001, while the signs of life were budding all around us, my husband and I learned that a life was beginning to form inside of me; our first child. After the results were confirmed by our physician we returned home filled with joy and excitement. In time we informed family and friends that we were expecting. Our daughters shared in our excitement and eagerly awaited the birth of their little brother/sister.

As the weeks drifted by, our excitement quickly faded as death and misery came knocking at our door. We received the heart breaking news that our baby was losing life as he/she was lodged in one of my fallopian tubes. We were grief-stricken to know that we were losing and eventually lost our first child. It seemed that all of this: life and death happened in just a twinkling of an eye. Heartbroken and disappointed my husband and I returned home still hopeful that additional children would be a part of our life. After sharing our loss with our daughters and others we continued on with life full of hope and anticipation of what was to come. Though I did not know at that time, this loss and brokenness was one of many that I would experience on my way to complete healing and deliverance.

Over the next few years each emotional attempt to conceive was met with a much greater degree of hurt and disappointment. The intensity of my infertility struggle not only affected my husband and me, but it spilled over onto our children and extended family. Even though the details of our struggles were not shared with them our families were always there standing in the gap to console and provide unconditional support to us.

****

In October of 2003, we learned that we were expecting our second child. Out of fear of premature excitement, my husband was hesitant to inform anyone that we were expecting. He was still holding on to the pain of our previous experience. Thus, we agreed to wait until Christmas Day to announce to our family that we were having a baby.

On the morning of December 23, 2003 my husband and I woke up excited and eager to start the day. We were feeling fantastic and looked forward to spending the day together as we prepared for Christmas with our families. It was early that morning while at a doctor's appointment that we received the unexpected news that for reasons unknown our child had taken a turn for the worst. The doctor advised us that it would take a drastic change, a medical miracle, for me to carry this child to term. My husband and I did not discuss the appointment much when we left the doctor's office but we both left there expecting and believing God for just that; a miracle.

After spending the rest of the morning and afternoon together my husband and I returned home in the evening as if nothing were wrong. Once the children were asleep, we wrapped a few Christmas gifts for them and placed them under the Christmas tree. I turned in a little earlier than normal while my husband continued with the Christmas preparations.

Around 10:00 p.m. that evening, I was awakened as a sharp pain in my abdomen hit me like a ton of bricks. It was a type of pain that I had never experienced before. I laid in bed refusing to accept what I thought was happening. I eventually crawled out of bed and made my way to our bathroom. I laid on the floor cradled in a fetal position, while biting down on the corner of the pillow I used to comfort my abdomen. Over the next two hours, I literally crawled alone between the bedroom and the bathroom denying the rupturing that was occurring on the inside of me. I did everything within my power to mask the pain in order to keep my husband, who still in the next room preparing for Christmas, from learning that the miracle we were hoping for was not going to happen.

The thought that kept playing itself over and over in my head was the pain we both felt and the tears we cried with our last failed pregnancy a little over two years ago. I could not bear to face the disappointment again knowing the high hopes we both had in the delivery of this child.

As I laid on the floor, I prayed and I prayed that God would have mercy on me and allow me to somehow carry this child to term. I murmured prayers like, *"If not for me, God, please save this child for my husband's sake."* I did not want God to punish my husband for the wrongs of my past. This was a barren situation that I created, not my husband. My biggest fear was that my husband's optimism in birthing a child with me would soon wear and he would regret ever having married me. So, I laid there in the darkness, hiding from the inevitable, wallowing in of the error of my ways in prayer. The more I prayed the greater the pain. Each of my petitions to God was met with a greater rupturing on the inside of me.

After a period of stillness, my husband approached the closed bathroom door and asked if everything was okay. I replied to him in a pained voice, *"I...am...fine,"* knowing full well that I was dying inside. Our child was losing life inside of my womb and so was I. I was so consumed with concern for how my husband was going to react to the seemingly impossibility of fathering a child through our marriage that it did not matter that a pool of blood was beginning to form inside of me. At that moment, I would have rather died than face the disappointment standing on the other side of that door. Thus, I continued to lie there, hoping that I would wake up to find it was all a dream.

Eventually, the pain got so bad that I could not make it back to my bed alone. I banged on the floor to get my husband's attention and he immediately came to my aid. He helped me back to the bed and without delay my husband placed a call to our physician. It was around 3:00 a.m. in the morning, so he had to leave a message with the after-hours answering service. Our physician was very responsive and promptly returned our call within a matter of minutes. After my husband explained our fears and the pain I was experiencing the doctor instructed us to meet him at his office when it opened at 8:00 a.m. He cautioned that if we could not make it through the next few hours, then we should go to the emergency room.

Six hours later, after one of the most sleepless nights of my life my husband carefully wheeled me into the doctor's office. After a brief exam and ultrasound our doctor advised us that our child was gone. Gone! He also advised that because my fallopian tube had ruptured and I was beginning to bleed internally he was immediately admitting me to the hospital to perform emergency surgery for my safety. A couple of hours later I found myself in a holding area, sprawled out yet again, on a cold surgical steel table, drifting off to sleep as bright reflector lights illuminated my body. I laid there wondering why my God had once again turned a deaf ear to my prayers.

After the surgery I woke up in a recovery room. The good news that we intended to share with our family during this season was now overtaken with bad news. It was now Christmas Eve and we did not want our daughters to know that I was in the hospital. We thought it would be too much for their young minds to understand. Thus, I called my sister, who was caring for them and explained what had occurred. Before ending the conversation, I asked my sister not to tell the girls what was going on because I did not want either of them to be worried. Next, my husband called his older brother to explain our loss. The anticipated joy and excitement that we thought we would experience on Christmas day when we announced to our families that I was pregnant was now replaced with the announcement of death.

Given the medical success of my surgery and the fact that it was Christmas Eve, our physician allowed me to return home that evening. I find it hard to consider the surgery a success since it did not change the fact that I loss our child. I spent Christmas and the next several days on bed rest. As I think back on this experience this was yet another step of brokenness that I had to endure on my journey of releasing the reins of my reproductive life to God's control.

****

A few weeks after losing our second child, my husband and I found ourselves being rooted in a wonderful church. We had always attended church regularly but this was the first church we joined as a family since our marriage. We found a place where we were both praising and worshiping God. We were experiencing a seemingly happy home life where we loved and supported one another, yet we were not in total agreement on whether or not we would continue in our hopes to parent children together. My husband appeared to become resigned to the belief that maybe it was not part of God's plan for us to have children. Naturally, this threatened the fiber of our marriage, particularly since we had previously professed our belief that God's *Word* did not exclude us as it relates to husbands and wives being fruitful.

Instead, my husband diverted his fatherly inclination toward being the best uncle possible (a godly example) to his younger nieces and nephews. When he first told me this I immediately recognized it as a loss of faith in the most intimate aspect of our marital relationship that would result in discontinuing all efforts to nourish the wifely vine attempting to bring forth children in his home (Psalms 128). My husband's resolve to lavish the fatherly love he embodied upon nieces and nephews told me that he still desperately wanted and deserved to have children to call his own. The difficulty for both of us was finding a way to overcome the pain and disappointment of our past. While my husband appeared to have given up hope, I pressed into God even the more in hopes that *HE* would move on our behalf. Why wouldn't *He*? I loved *Him* and worshiped *Him* with all my heart. What else did I need to do to prove my faithfulness? I simply could not understand why God appeared to separate *Himself* from me in this lone area of my life.

****

Several months later, during a worship service I found myself seeking prayer from a married expectant mother in response to an altar call led by our pastor. The memory of this day will never escape me. The sanctuary was filled with God's presence as melodious music set the atmosphere for humility and surrender. Our pastor spoke encouraging words and opened the altar to all married women who had a desire to conceive but for whatever reason had not been able to. During the altar call Pastor asked all the married women in the church who were currently expecting a child to come to the altar and prayer for all the barren women seeking prayer. When at last the call was settled and all the married women trying to conceive were summoned to approach the altar, I hesitated. The memory of my marred past, woven with the stench of defeat consumed me. Instead, I engaged in spiritual warfare with the enemy who heralded in my ear, "the damage you intended to be permanent in your womb is just that, permanent."

The enemy had me convinced that I would be lying and giving myself false hope if I responded to the altar call. My husband, who was standing with me as our pastor was ministering this altar call, encouraged me to have faith in God's *Word* spoken through our pastor. While the enemy continued to ring the words *"liar…liar…liar"* into my ear, my husband whisper to me, *"aren't you going?"* and with a gentle nudge he encouraged me to step towards the altar. These steps were the first steps of faith taken by me towards escaping from my wilderness. In fact, this was a major move in the right direction towards my eventual recognition of the heightened offense I had committed. With God's revelation of my wrong, I humbled myself in repentance and vowed to do all in my power to ratify my earlier act of disobedience.

While at the altar, the Holy Spirit freed me from a darkness that had hovered over me for more than 14 years. I repented for allowing my defeated human nature to interfere with the value I placed on being the life-giving vessel I was designed to be. I repented for taking my reproductive destiny into my own hands. I even repented for not realizing that restoring my fertility should have been for the purpose of returning to God that which I had taken from *Him*. It was on that day that I was led to re-dedicate my life and reproductive destiny to God. I proclaimed that the power of life and death was in *His* hands. I exalted God as the giver of life and availed my body to *Him* as a conduit for which to reproduce life in *His* image, in *His* timing and for *His* purpose. I left the altar and sanctuary on that day with God at the helm of my life, delivered from the sins of my past and totally restored in right standing with *Him*.

****

As I continued to press into God's *Word* (the bible) for growth and knowledge, I stumbled upon these words: *"Behold, the Lord's hand is not shortened, that it cannot save, or his ear dull, that it cannot hear; but your iniquities have made a separation between you and your God, and your sins have hid his face from you so that he does not hear."* It was at this point in my journey that I realized that God had not closed *His* ear to my prayers. However, my prayers had been hindered because of my sin and disobedience. The reason I could not grasp this before is because I had focused all my attention on my current lifestyle, not the things of my past life. Consequently, I was seeking the peace of God, but had not made peace with God. I wanted *His* blessings but was not repentant of the things I had done to position me into a separated condition. For years this separation confirmed itself in my life with each failed attempt at conception and with each failed attempt to carry our child to term. Thank God for revelation, because it was at this time that *His Word* was made clear and I was

118

even the more repentant for things I had done in the past, known and unknown that were contrary to *His Word*.

Less than a year after the altar call that lead to my earnest repentance, my husband and I learned that we were expecting our third child. The doctor told us that everything looked fine. Physically, we did not have to worry about manifestation of any of our previous issues. I was instructed to start taking prenatal vitamins and all ultrasounds up to that point looked perfect. Spiritual repentance and God's forgiveness placed me in right standing with *Him*. God's promises were being fulfilled in our lives. *He* had breathed life into my once barren womb.

****

As the trees of my wilderness began to part and the sky was beginning to appear, only God knew that I would be tested once again to ascertain the depth of my true faith in *Him*. My test tracked me down like a high powered arrow drawn from a finely crafted bow of the master archer *Himself*. The potency of the arrow plunged into my heart with these trying words levied from the lips of *His* messenger (a nurse) who called me on my job and stated, *"I am so very sorry, but your blood work indicates that your pregnancy is dissipating."*

"Dissipating? What do you mean?" I asked. The nurse replied, *"The results indicate that you have lost your child...I'm sorry."* After a short pause she goes on to tell me to stop taking my prenatal vitamins and to come in next week to speak with my doctor. Realizing the devastating news that she had delivered, she asked me if I needed anything or if there was anything she could do. The comfort of a nurse was not what I needed. I began to ask myself if I had truly handed my reproductive destiny over to God? Did I truly believe that God would deliver the breath of life necessary to emit life from the valley of death that *He* had formed in my womb? Whose word would I choose to believe, God's or man's?

At that moment, I stood up, walked away from my desk and began to pace the halls. I soon found myself locked away in a restroom stall located in the basement of the office building I worked in. I began to pray as God unraveled *His Word* inside of me. I began to speak life and words of prophesy over the seed God had placed into my womb. I encouraged myself that the hand of the Lord was upon me; and according to *His Word, He* would not leave nor forsake me. I spoke God's *Word* into the life of my unborn child, and the miraculous work that God had ordained for him/her to complete here on this earth.

After sharing the lab results with my husband, I demonstrated my faith in God daily, by going against the advice of medical personnel. I continued to take prenatal vitamins and continued to nurture the seed that the nurse had told me was dead; dissipating. I could feel God's strength band around us as my husband and I prayed, and he anointed my belly. Though very supportive and caring, my husband was admittedly very delicate in everything he said and did during this period.

A week later, as we sat in our doctor's office, we were informed by our doctor that he had just learned that the lab made an unexplainable error in reading my lab results. After another ultrasound, it was confirmed that our child was healthy and growing at a rapid rate! Praise God! I still remember the look of amazement on the nurse's face when she told me that I should start back taking my prenatal vitamins and I responded to her, *"I never stopped."*

Over the next few months, we continued to lift our child up in prayer. On November 30, 2005, God breathed yet another breath of life into her nostrils, as we were blessed with a healthy baby girl, our gift from God. We thankfully named her, Madison Oluchi (Madison meaning, gift from God; and Oluchi meaning God's handiwork.)

Today our bright and brilliant daughter leads us in prayer and knows that she is God's child. Among the first words she ever spoke, she clearly pronounced the name, *"Jesus"* and made references to *"Heaven."* Just the other day, while at her pre-school orientation, my husband and I were in the classroom speaking with the school's director, when we heard a group of kids coming down the hallway. With the group of kids we heard the sweetest angelic sounds of a three-year-old child singing *"Glory to God on High ... Let all of the angels sing..."* In amazement, the director, with my husband and I in tow, rushed out of the classroom to catch a glimpse of this precious gift singing about her heavenly *Father*. I am so godly proud to say that, yes this little angel is ours...our now three-year-old gift from God.

It was similar moments like this experienced with our daughter and her unexplainable knowledge of Jesus, that inspired me to write a short story several months ago entitled, *Lent Soul*. I have summarized a few excerpts from that story below:

Lent Soul

Today was destined to be a beautiful day in heaven. It was the day that Lent Soul, along with many other beaming souls in heaven, would enter the observation corridors to glean the lives of parents God had appointed to serve as conduits for their descent into the world. Lent Soul was particularly excited about this opportunity to observe his parents, for it would be his parents who would be the determining factor in whether or not Lent Soul would have an opportunity to fulfill the purpose for which he was created.

Lent Soul realized that God created him to accomplish a great work in the world. In order for Lent Soul to accomplish that great work, he would have to descend from heaven onto the earth and be clothed in flesh and blood just like the Lord Jesus did thousands of years ago. There is certainly no comparison between the work of Jesus and that of Lent Soul, but both had assignments of great importance. Lent Soul's mission was to bring a greater understanding to the Body of Christ of the importance of preserving godliness in the world through the reproduction of godly offspring.

In order for Lent Soul to be successful in his mission, he had to be born to God-fearing parents who would reverence Lent Soul as a soul lent by God for nurturing to God's glory. This nurturing would ensure Lent Soul's biblical upbringing and preparation for God's use. His parents would be the water on the seed that would bring to Lent Soul's remembrance the great calling on his life in the event Lent Soul should go astray...

Lent Soul prayed daily that his chosen parents embodied the belief of the virgin mother Mary; the humility and desire of the barren mother Hannah; and the unity of oneness, patience and faith that was demonstrated in the lives of Isaac and Rebecca. Lent Soul's prayers went deep into the very fiber of the issues that his life on earth was destined to bring to deliverance. Lent Soul was very passionate about his mission and was fully aware of the enormity of his great calling.

Daily Lent Soul could peep out of heaven's window and literally see the waxing of moral decline embraced by young tainted souls inhibiting the earth. It was God who revealed to Lent Soul that there had been a rapid decline in the nurturing and developing of bright souls toward the fulfillment of their purpose in life once they descended onto the earth. Lent Soul could not fathom how so many of the bright souls he once knew in heaven could descend onto the earth and go astray

Together, God and Lent Soul observed how non-believing populations were producing far more children than Christian populations. Year, after year, after year, fewer children from Christian homes were entering the first grade. Many of the children entering preschool were born to unmarried women who were birthing twice as many children as married women in the Body of Christ. Oh, yes, this was of great concern to God and Lent Soul because a rapid decline of fertility levels among Christians not only threatened the destiny of great souls like Lent Soul but also served as a direct threat to the future heritage of the church.

"Lent Soul, your time has come," an angel called and the birds of heaven began to sing.

****

The excerpt from the *Lent Soul* story is design bring spiritual relevancy to the practice of voluntary sterilization in the Body of Christ. My concern is that if God has commanded us to be fruitful and multiply, and if it is *He* that opens a womb and allows conception; and closes a womb to prevent it; is it not an act of rebellion when we attempt to thwart *His* plans for our reproductive life? When we take our reproductive destiny out of God's hands we are choosing where and under which circumstances we **will not** acknowledge *His* Lordship.

When we attempt to prevent conception, are we not *"leaning on our own understanding instead of leaning on the Word of God?"* Medicine and technology now allows individuals to circumvent the blessings of family and substitute our own logic for God's wisdom. We can now prevent conception to a reasonable degree of certainty. No matter what reasons we give, when we take matters into our own hands, we are acting in rebellion to God's command to be fruitful and multiply. We are also usurping *His* sovereignty over the child bearing process.

If Christians truly believe that and the Bible is wholly true all of the time, then how can we selectively seek to take the control of conception away from the Lord? The Bible says, children are to be considered a blessing and a gift from the Lord. The natural order of things dictates that when a marriage occurs, children will usually be produced. If Christian men and women were truly being fruitful and multiplying, how would that change our schools and communities?

As Christians, we are expected to make deliberate decisions with a mind of Christ. It is the black and white letter of the law that we ascribe to; choose a blessed and fruitful life of fertility or choose a cursed life of bewilderment and elective barrenness (*see Deuteronomy 30:19*). The choice is ours. However, we must realize that along with this freedom of choice comes the burden of consequence which many of us are not prepared to reap. While many of us understand this process, there are those of us who naturally look for "wiggle room" when we encounter biblical scripture that apply to our lives and it does not say what we want it to say. This is particularly the case when it comes to birth control and sterility measures. The problem with this flesh driven response is that there is overwhelming evidence against wiggle room on the issue of preventing conception. God's *Word* is the one constant in this world that is true all the time. Either you believe all of it or none of it.

The ladies of old used to sing a song that said, *"Lord prepare me, to be a sanctuary, pure and holy tried and true. And with Thanksgiving, I'll be a living sanctuary, Lord for you."* I never truly understood this collection of words until now. Through trials, tests and now triumphs I realize that my body is a temple for the dwelling of the Holy Spirit, whom I have received from God. I now know that I am not my own, but have been bought at a price paid with the blood of Jesus Christ. This knowledge has caused me to place God in *His* rightful place in my life by honoring *Him* with my body at all times (1 Corinthians 6:19-20 (NIV).

PRESSING THE MARK

by Toni Emehel

The bible encourages us that the fruit of our womb is God's reward. When married couples elect to live barren lifestyles, what are they really saying to God? I am reminded of the story written in the book of Genesis of a man called Onan, who married his deceased brother's wife. Onan wanted the virtues of marriage but refused to conceive with his bride. God's reaction to Onan's displeasing behavior gives us some idea of the heightened level of discontentment God experiences when husbands and wives intentionally engage in forbearances of this nature. Read Genesis 38:6-10 and allow God to speak to your heart.

1. Why did Onan's actions displease God?

2. Is it possible that Onan's behavior demonstrated signs of an idolatrous lifestyle? (see 1 John 2:15-17)

3. What about your own lifestyle? Are there any pleasures in your life that continually cause you to disregard God's intended purpose and plan for your life?

PONDERING THOUGHTS

What makes you uncomfortable about leaving it to God to determine when and how many children you should have? Pray about your current reproductive practices. Let God lead you in determining what actions you need to take to fully put *HIM* in control of your reproductive destiny.

ACKNOWLEDGMENTS

Acknowledgments

This project owes its life to the encouragement and support of our spouses, family and closest friends without which we might not have been able to complete our mission. The writing of this book is the first of many Wilderness Women projects to come in our quest to elevate the spirit, free the soul and share the realness of God's grace.

— Wilderness Women

I am personally indebt to many people for their love and support with this endeavor, but none more that my husband, Johneric. You are truly God's gift to me! Thank you for your blessings and support in sharing our story. I love you and owe you a debt of gratitude for your patience in the development of this God ordained work.

To the "Wilderness Women," this book was waiting to be written for such a time as this. Millions of people in this world are troubled and in need of hope for a successful future. Through sharing a piece of your life, you have provided an impassioned prescription destined to deliver curative care. This book is a tribute to your openness and honesty. Partnering with you on this project made writing a pleasure.

— Toni

BOOK CLUB RESOURCES

If your Book Club would like to schedule a conference call with Toni Emehel or one of the contributing authors of *Wilderness Women*: *Live to tell the story*, please email us at: EdmondEmehelGroupe@msn.com with the following information:

- Name of Book Club

- Number of Book Club Members

- City and State where the Book Club is located

- Contact Person: name, phone number and email address

- Comments and preferred meeting times

While we cannot guarantee times requested, authors will make every effort to fit your book clubs conference call into their schedule.

...this book was waiting to be written for such a time as this. Millions of people in this world are troubled and in need of hope for a successful future.

—*Toni Emehel*

AFTERWORD

Afterword

Trusting in God is not an enjoyable experience. Some would call it a wilderness experience, beset with hardship, uncertainty and pain. As best I can describe it…it feels like you are walking through a forest of land mines and trying to navigate your way through without being annihilated. Your emotional senses strengthen and you begin to hear things with a heightened awareness. If you are not careful you will begin to focus on the wrong sounds and completely miss the voice of God that is there to guide you.

When we find ourselves in a state of bewilderment, it is because God has allowed the situation in order to build our trust in *Him.* God has a plan for our lives that involves living a life of peace, but we must first seek *Him.* There is a passage of scripture in the book of Jeremiah that affirms God's desire to bring us through life's wilderness situations closer to *Him: "For I know the thoughts that I think toward you, says the LORD, thoughts of peace and not of evil, to give you a future and a hope. Then you will call upon Me and go and pray to Me, and I will listen to you. And you will seek Me and find Me, when you search for Me with all your heart. I will be found by you, says the LORD, and I will bring you back from your captivity; I will gather you from all the nations and from all the places where I have driven you, says the LORD, and I will bring you to the place from which I cause you to be carried away captive (v.29:11-14 NIV)."*

The only way to escape the wilds of life is to trust in God, have faith in *His Word* and trust in *His* guiding light (i.e. the Holy Spirit) to show us the way. Don't be like the children of Israel, who took 40 years to establish their trust in God. The sooner you put your trust in *Him;* the sooner *He* will set you free. Surrender your life to God and allow *Him* to show you the way out of your wilderness!

Until we meet again, be empowered and tread in peace.

— *Toni Emehel*

When we find ourselves in a state of bewilderment, it is because God has allowed the situation in order to build our trust in Him.

—Toni Emehel

ABOUT THE AUTHOR

Contact the Author

It is important that I hear how, *Wilderness Women: Live to tell the story* has had a positive impact on your life. Blog Toni at:

www.ToniEmehel.blogspot.com

or send your testimony to:

Toni Emehel

P.O Box 7252

Charlotte, NC 28241

A new voice…A fresh inspiration

Toni Emehel, the visionary author behind *Wilderness Women: Live to tell the story,* lives in the suburbs of Charlotte, North Carolina with husband and soul mate Johneric C. Emehel. Toni is the mother of three dynamic and fun spirited daughters; Tressica Denise, Jessica Laneé and Madison Oluchi. She embraces her role as grandmother of two adorable grandchildren; Isaiah Landon and Brie Antoinette. Toni devoted twenty-one years to working in corporate America before God called Toni to devote her life to building *His* Kingdom by focusing on her family, which spawned the writing, *"Fleeing from Woman,"* and ultimately the vision for orchestrating *Wilderness Women: Live to tell the story.* Toni has a dedicated heart for God and for touching the lives of people with God's word. She has humbled herself for God's use through the sharing of the gifts and talents God has blessed her with. From outreach to in-reach, Toni shares God's word straight from her heart with love, humor and transparency. Toni cares enough to openly make use of tough issues affecting her own life to bring God's message in a manner that brings relevancy to others.

> *"No matter what cards you have been dealt in life, the choice is yours to overcome or to be defeated."*
>
> —*Sheria Lofton*

BONUS CHAPTER

BLOG DISCUSSION

And she spoke these words, saying, "Sometimes I feel like nobody understands me. Sometimes, I feel like the odd one with no body to care for me. Sometimes, I feel like an abandoned child lost, unloved, with no one to talk to. Sometimes I feel like I'm stuck in a box screaming for help, but nobody can hear me. People are there, family, friends, church leaders…looking dead at me yet they cannot hear my cries nor understand my pain.

Yes sometimes…I feel like nobody understands me. That's just the way I feel. It's the way I feel now and perhaps always if people who say they care never grow to understand."

—Jessica L. Wallace

Voiced from the pages of a young girl's journal, this crystalline expression is the epitome of pain lurking in the lives of many women and young adolescent girls today. As a woman, I realize that there are diverse life situations and cultural factors that give way to wilderness experiences in a woman's life. All too often, when going through these wilderness experiences it seems that no one around you truly understands your (sometimes) paralyzing pain. As a result, it seems that those who claim to care about us seemingly jump on the bandwagon in support of the very issue that thrust you into a wilderness state or condition. What's more is that it seems like repeat behaviors continue to contribute to and/or create new wilderness situations that keep us from escaping the wilderness environment.

Our challenge as women is to educate those around us by identifying the specific nature of those "things" that contribute to, catapult us into and/or create wilderness environments in our lives. We all know that ultimately, God is in control of everything and nothing happens unless *He* allows it to. However, speaking out on the issues that most affect us will hopefully keep those closest to us from being used as instruments of the enemy to bring about life situations that were never meant for us to experience. When we get caught up in a "thing" out of relationship (and not because of God) that is when God allows us to enter the forest.

So, my question to the "Wilderness Women" is: how can you help others to understand the sensitive nature of an ordinary woman and the seemingly "little things" that create wilderness environments in her life?

—Toni Emehel

Reply by WildernessWoman: Sat 10/25/08 at 9:24 a.m.

In looking back, to recall a wilderness period, I have concluded that all of life is lived *in the wilderness.* In the beginning God created (a) Genesis 1:1a … and God saw that it was good (b) Genesis 1:25. God created man and woman and put them in the beautiful Garden of Eden and supplied all they needed…PERFECTION!

We know how that ended … and man has been in the wilderness since. This wilderness is beautiful and diverse; it is breathtaking, even through storming weather. It has all we need, but it is no longer pleasant, peaceful, or pretty all the time… because of sin and self will. Our wilderness is what it is because of the choices we make, as well as disobedience and selfishness. My wildernesses are those events or periods of time when I made choices that thrust me outside the Garden, away from God. Once outside the garden, I did or dealt with stuff in ways that came between me and God.

My childhood was good because it was what it was, and we did what we did, because parents do what they have learned, or how they interpret what they see others do in rearing their children. My early life in the wilderness for the most part, was dull and ordinary as I look back, but we had a very good life growing up.

Believing I was supposed to be good (obedient, honest and kind) was far most on my mind and I was determined not to embarrass the family or myself. Little did I know, I could not be good all the time, under all circumstances, because of what happened in the Garden of Eden and there were always choices to make.

Reply by Sanderson: Sat 10/25/08 6:20 p.m.

There have been plenty of sorry women to pull a good man down and like wise with a number of good women being destroyed by the schisms of trifling men. Check yourself to ensure you are doing your part. When in doubt, consult the owner's manual (the Bible) derived by the *One* who created you, God. The Bible provides us with a good source of wisdom to learn all the characteristics of a good man as well as virtues needed to become a virtuous woman. Empower yourself with God's Word and stop fooling yourself by thinking that your way is your own. It not as much about you as you think. Once you realize it's all about God your life will be much better. Be blessed!

Reply by Watson_rl: Sun 11/30/08 at 9:28 p.m. There was a time in my life when I felt like a caged animal, craving to be free. I was in a relationship that was not fulfilling, but I didn't know how to break free. I wanted to scream, but I couldn't find my voice. I felt that I was in the wilderness all alone. I began to ask myself, what am I afraid of? Am I afraid of being alone? Had I lost my voice because I was afraid of what I might say? I began to take a close look at myself and take inventory. I was educated, beautiful, open, honest, dependable, lovable, sexy, and the list goes on…By the time I finished taking stock in myself, I surmised that anyone who found themselves in my company must be blessed! Because I'm a precious jewel to behold and need to be treated as such. I realized that not everyone deserved my time and my company. I learned to love myself and spend time with myself. When I look in the mirror, I focused on my beauty. I take myself shopping, to the movies, out to dinner and pamper myself every chance I get. Nobody can love me like I can. Because I love myself so much, I began to speak up about what I was feeling. Yeah, I may have hurt some feelings, but I had to be clear about what I needed for my own happiness. I became very discriminate about who I spent my time with after I freed myself from that cage I had built around myself…Yeah, I built it, so it was my responsibility to tear it down…Learn to take responsibility for yourself, it can be empowering!

Reply by S. Lofton: Sat 11/22/08 at 5:48 p.m. Beautiful Flower Thanks to the men that love us through thick and thin. For you see, that we have value within. We are precious and delicate like a little flower. So, please don't devour your beautiful flower. Be gentle with your flower, help her blossom. Help her to be all that God created her to be. Not hindering or causing her to wither away in dismay. Water her with your love. Shower her with encouragement. Never compare her to Rose, Dahlia, Lily, and Daisy, for she is unique in her own special way. Most of all love her very deeply.

If by chance this flower is placed in the wrong hands, she will be used and abused and picked apart emotionally and physically until she will never bloom or blossom into her full potential. So, if you don't love her don't waste her space. Your flower has been through a lot and God will deal with the matters of your heart.

Reply by V. Arleen: Tues 10/28/2008 at 8:25 p.m. Gentlemen, the Bible says that life and death is in the power of the tongue. Before you say I love you to a woman be sure that you are ready, willing and able to back those words up with the corresponding actions. Know what it means to have the 1 Corinthians 13 kind of love. Know what it means to love as Christ loved the church. Using words of love without understanding its meaning and without the works to prove it is manipulation and emotional abuse. Just like faith without works is dead so is love without the actions to prove it. Using these words improperly can cause the death of a woman's trust. Watch your mouth! Ladies, love is explainable and it is not blind. If a man cannot explain to you and show you his love in action, do not give him the liberty to manipulate and abuse your heart and your emotions. You must guard your heart for out of it flow the issues of life.

Reply by V. Arleen: Thurs 10/30/2008 9:26 p.m. Gents, every woman needs a man who can cover her as a true leader and head. Before you progress a relationship to marriage, be honest with the woman and yourself as to your ability to cover her. Make sure you have the needed equipment for the woman you choose. Don't marry a woman who needs a king size comforter if all you have is a receiving blanket or a twin size sheet. You will kill her potential and your relationship if you force her to curl up or shrink in order to fit under your covering. It is like buying a house or car that is out of your financial league. Eventually the debt will catch up to you and the possessions become more of a burden than a joy. In too many cases the final result could be foreclosure or repossession. Grow your covering first then take the bride. Ladies, beware of a man who is not himself under spiritual covering. A man without accountability to a covering does not understand the purpose of submission, power and authority. Examine his own covering for holes, appropriate size and accountability before you submit your life in marriage to any man.

Reply by V. Arleen: Sat 11/01/2008 10:00 a.m. Gents, The Bible says that the enemy comes to steal, kill and destroy. But Jesus came that we might have life and that more abundantly. If your relationship with a woman kills, steals or destroys anything good and right in the eyes of God in that woman's body, soul or spirit, you are an instrument of evil. Leave the woman alone or repent and change sides now! If you are causing abundance and growth in the body, soul and spirit of a woman, keep up the good work! God is using you for His glory! Ladies, take note. This is a sure way to tell if a man was sent into your life by God or the enemy. Keep your eyes wide open!

Reply by Blkcoffee10: Wed 11/28/08 3:18 p.m. To determine the nature of a woman who creates a wilderness environment for herself, you must first look at her character traits. Is she the type of person that has an easy going or passive spirit? If so, I am sorry to say but; in my personal opinion this is the start to her wilderness. I say this, because in today's society people have no respect for the easy going/meek spirited woman. They have respect for her as long as her spirit is going to benefit them. In the bible this spirit falls along the lines of being hopeful or optimistic, thinking the best of all situations. This is usually the thinking of the easygoing woman. I know, because I'm one of them. Romans 8:25 states: "But if we hope for that we see not, then do we with patience wait for it?" Patience as seen in spirit of an easy going woman can be seen in the manner in which she handles difficult matters. She can be seen going through a difficult situation with calm endurance without complaining, losing self control or even acknowledging the fact that the situation is getting on her nerves. If this is you, you are setting yourself up for big disappointments.

If you knowingly do not open your mouth and cry out in hard times you could be the cause of your own wilderness. Let people know your feelings. Don't keep them bottled up inside. I know that in the bible that Psalm 33:20 says, "Our soul waiteth for the Lord: he is our help and our shield." This is oh so true, but we also have to realize that times have changed over the years and technically our roles as women have changed too. The weight of the world is on our shoulders and societal norms have allowed our men to skirt their duties and responsibilities as men. Now, don't get me wrong, we still have some good God-Fearing men in our society, but you need to realize that the pickin's are slim. Secondly, in order to escape the experience of being a wilderness woman, you have to be purposeful in everything that you do. You have to know God's will in your life and work toward accomplishing it. If you find your purpose and keep your focus then

God will order your steps. This can only be done through prayer. Find you a prayer closet and visit it regularly.

And another thing, don't hesitate to fellowship with other Christian sisters. A lot of times God put these women in our paths to share a Word directly from Him to you. These sisters are sent your way to be supportive, to give you strength and encourage you in times of troubles. Galatians 6:2 "Bear ye one another's burdens, and so fulfill the law of Christ."

Thirdly, I would recommend to all women that we need to be selfish from time to time. I have learned that we should never selflessly give our all to anyone but God. A lot of times, people tend to take our kindness for weakness and will take advantage of you if you let them. We have to tell ourselves that it is all about us and God. If you have a spouse who has a personal relationship with God, then he comes next. Last, but not least, if you have small children, then it should be about God, you and your children. We as women have to secure perseverance in our life. Meaning that we need to be able to cope with stress and accomplish God's intended work for us. Perseverance is a must for the wilderness woman.

Fourthly, pray and ask God for wisdom and the gift of discernment. The ability to make good judgment is highly essential for a woman going through the wilderness. We need to be able to tell the difference between good and bad. This would save us a lot of heartache and illness in our lives. We need to know when it's time to cry out for help and we need to know when to let go of the things that are hurting us. A lot of us do not realize that we have help-lines right before our eyes. We do not have to go through life hurting, feeling lonely, ashamed or being sick in some situation that we should have ridded ourselves of a long time ago. The Lord said for us to do His will, however; he didn't intend for us to be fools. I now realize that I could have saved myself from a lifetime of taking medications if I had only spoke out when times were rough and walked away when my instinct told me to. Take heed and make it one less wilderness story to be told!

In closing, I would like to say to you look to the hills from whence cometh your help and realize that all of your help comes from the Lord, not man. Be blessed!

Reply by J. Little: Thurs 11/20/08 10:11 p.m. You finally get that ride you've been wanting. You make sure it stays clean inside and out. Of course you have to shine those rims every weekend. Cheap gas in that beauty? Unheard of. The oil gets changed every 3000 miles without failure.

One day you get in, turn it on and the engine light comes on. This is a warning sign that something is wrong. You don't want to keep driving with that engine light on because one problem may lead to another. And you know if you don't deal with it, eventually the car will break down. So, what do you do? You take it to the mechanic as soon as possible. The mechanic tells you the problem. If you don't have the money on hand, you will whip that credit card out with no problem because you've got to get your baby up and running again.

My brothers, don't you see your spouses' engine lights on? Stop ignoring it and hoping it will go away. It won't. The light may go off for a moment but the problem is still there. Internal damages are still being done and one problem is leading to another. Deal with the situation. You do it for that ride. Isn't she more important? Don't you want your baby up and running again?

Reply by TMassey: Wed 12/03/08 at 2:18 p.m.
In a lot of today's churches we find a lot of leaders who are highly educated, dignified and yes, snooty. It is an honor to be highly educated and ok to be dignified as long as it is all about Christ and not self fulfilling. Snooty to society on the other hand may appear as you being unapproachable.

Check yourself, are you unapproachable? Do you mainly find yourself mingling with the "in crowd," those of your standards or do you have some mission relationships with the "out crowd," those who are in need of a witness? Take a scroll down memory lane when you saw someone who attended your church searching for an answer to life's struggles and yet they did not dress, smell, speak, pray or quote the scriptures like you. Did you approach them to say hello or make them feel comfortable and a part of the worship experience or did you just ignore their presence? So many churches claim an open door policy for membership, yet if you are not a part of the "in crowd", you are ignored as a member.

Too often this leads a person free to leave and in search of other endeavors. Remember when you were a babe in Christ how you needed the support of others to mentor you, to pray with you or just to lend an ear to listen to you to help you stay on the right track? Now you are Pastor, Deacon, Mother, etc and all of a sudden everyone else appears beneath you. Let's get back to the basics when the church members were considered Christian families in and out of the church.

Never forget a higher elevation means broader challenges. Remember Jesus mingled with the broken, the ones that no one else wanted to be bothered with, yet He had the highest elevation of anyone that ever walked this earth. This is what made him so special to mankind. Let's get back to the basics of witnessing, mentoring and winning souls, showing genuine love and building Christian relationships so that we are about our Father's business.

Reply by LClay09: Sat 03/07/09 at 10:04 a.m.

Pillow Talk for the Soul: In this world today there are many uncertainties, yet, there is one thing that still gets better with time and that is the art of love. What love is or isn't -- is more or less what you make it. A wilderness woman needs to experience love in its many facets to appreciate the fullness of what it could be.   Share your thoughts on the metaphors of Love.

Metaphors of Love...

Love is not just limited to mere words on a card or an exquisite stone set into the finest of metals. But yet it is built on trust, mutual respect and valuing one another standing together and facing the odds of this world.

Love is as musical rhythms, energetically and uniquely woven through the fibers of its lovers' hearts. It is when soul mates have been forced into unexpected separations that their hearts grow fonder.

Love is as a piece of coal chiseled with precision, to become a pristine diamond. It is the architect's building with every element carefully designed to produce a masterful structure second to none.

Love is as the finest of wines, cultured with time by the careful attention of its makers. It is a promised kept, full of trust and hope.

Love is as flowers in a garden, each when embraced with passion and tender loving care will bloom abundantly. It is that harvest when cultivated and planted on fertile ground begins to yield bountiful fruit.

Reply by LClay09: Tues 03/10/09 at 11:34 a.m.

Pillow Talk for the Soul: A wilderness Woman needs to be showered with love as she finds her way on this journey. What advice would you give regarding establishing boundaries in a relationship?

The Love toolkit…

Spending time with those that don't Value you is a waste of time and energy. Get rid of the losers, God has planned for you to have someone that places your value far above rubies.

A love that is filled with spontaneity is exciting and refreshing; it prevents the relationship from growing stale and becoming undesirable.

Love is a process that occurs over time. In a marriage relationship, don't be afraid to pursue him and give him the love he needs, for in so doing, you will reciprocate the love you need, thereby cultivating a love with an unbreakable bond. Enjoy the process for as it develops it will become what you both desire.

If this is the love that God has intended for you allow God to be the 3-strain cord that creates the unbreakable union, for a 3-strain cord is not easily broken. When God is the center of your lives, you will see good success.

Be careful of sharing intimate pillow talk conversation, or seeking relationship advice from the unmarried, the unwise and envious. Those that may have never experience a harmonious Eden relationship may suggest that it cannot exist. Yes I must admit there is work involved, as with any relationship you will occasionally disagree; but as you become adaptable to one another, you'll learn how to respectable and embrace the differences.